The Preacher
Volume 3

Variety In Preaching

Brian Galliers

ISBN 1 85852 174 2

© 2000 Trustees for Methodist Church Purposes

Scripture quotations, unless otherwise stated, are from the Holy Bible, New International Version. Copyright © 1973, 1978, 1984 by International Bible Society. Used by permission of Hodder & Stoughton Ltd, a member of the Hodder Headline Plc Group. All rights reserved.

All rights reserved. No part of this publication may be reproduced, stored in a retrieval system, transmitted, in any form or by any means, electronic, mechanical, photocopying, recording or otherwise, without the prior permission of Foundery Press, 20 Ivatt Way, Peterborough PE3 7PG

GENERAL INTRODUCTION

Preaching is a very particular form of communication which has always been important in the life of the Christian Church. At the beginning of the twenty-first century we are undergoing a revolution in the varieties, method and speed of our communications. Preachers of all denominations, ordained and lay, undertake this calling with an awareness that we preach in a changing context.

The Preacher's Library is designed to help us to think through, perhaps in some cases reassess, why we preach, how we preach, and to whom we preach. Some of the volumes in this series will take a fresh look at familiar issues, such as how preachers should approach various parts of the Bible, how we understand and express our doctrinal inheritance and the variety of styles in which preaching can be done. Other volumes will introduce issues which may be less familiar to many of us, such as the significance of our cultural context or the way in which the self-understanding of a woman preacher has important things to say to all preachers. Some of these books will offer direct help in the practice of preaching. Others will deal with issues which, although they appear more theoretical, impinge upon the preacher's task and on which we therefore need to have reflected if we are to preach with integrity in today's world.

All the writers in this series, lay and ordained, women and men, are recognised preachers within their own denominations and write with the needs of their colleagues firmly in mind. These books will avoid academic jargon, but they will not avoid dealing with difficult issues. They are offered to other preachers in the belief that as we deepen our thinking and hone our skills God's people will be blessed and built up to the glory of God.

In *Variety in Preaching*, Brian Galliers shares some of the fruits of his long and distinguished preaching ministry, exercised in a wide variety of settings. In a straightforward and practical manner he helps us reflect on such questions as variety of sermon length, use of biblical material, the different types of congregations we may face and the varying settings in which sermons are preached.

Michael J Townsend

CONTENTS

Chapter   **Page**

1   The Kingdom of Good News   1

2   Variety in Length   5

3   Variety in Approach   24

4   Variety of Purpose   53

5   Variety of People and Places   70

6   Message and Witness   82

1

THE KINGDOM OF GOOD NEWS

There was a time when the profile of the Methodist Church in central London was defined by the three names of Weatherhead, Sangster and Soper. Dr Leslie Weatherhead, minister at the City Temple, was famous as a popular preacher whose interest was in pastoral psychology; Dr William Sangster, at the Westminster Central Hall, was an evangelical; and Dr Donald Soper, at the Kingsway Hall, was a Christian socialist well-known for his speaking in the open air on Tower Hill and in Hyde Park. They were good colleagues, though very different in character and gifts. It was said of them that 'Leslie loves the people, Will loves the Lord, and Donald loves an argument.'

Those differences highlight the fact that there is a multitude of ways of proclaiming the good news about Jesus Christ. It has always been so. Matthew, Luke and John wrote their gospels in differing styles, with varied readerships in view. Paul and the writer to the Hebrews set out the significance of Jesus quite differently, whilst the Revelation of John had yet another approach. Our personalities and particular appreciation of the gospel message make a difference; and the people whom we are addressing and the situations in which they find themselves will also determine the way in which we present the message.

We are to look at variety in preaching in a number of ways. One issue is the *length* of the sermon. There is no God-given standard: we are to take the time that is necessary and appropriate, but no more. Another area is the *basis* on which we preach: will the starting point be a Bible word or passage, or will it arise out of a topical or experiential demand? Then there are *types* of sermon. Weatherhead, Sangster or Soper each had distinctive styles in setting out their message, but within those styles would operate from time to time in quite different ways. There must also be the consideration of the *people* and their settings, which will demand a sensitive and varied response from the preacher.

We are in the business of offering good news. Contrary to what many outside the Church may assume, we are not trying to cramp their enjoyment of life, nor setting out to offer 'good advice'. Nor is our task that of claiming that we have the answer to any and every situation. What we do possess should be an assurance that Jesus Christ is alive, and that in his life, death and resurrection two thousand years ago God offered himself to humankind in a unique and significant way. Mark comes straight to the point as he begins his account of Jesus' ministry, stating in the first sentence of his book that he is writing about the 'gospel' (which literally means good news) about Jesus, the Son of God. Mark has no doubts about the nature of what he is offering. He goes on to describe the way in which Jesus' message is centred on the 'kingdom', the rule of God over the hearts of men and women. It was a matter of saying 'Danger – God at work', much as we might be informed by a sign by the roadside today.

Jesus' own message was set out in a variety of ways, sometimes in teaching or preaching, sometimes in theological discussion; and to the dimension of speaking he added that of action. When God speaks, things happen; and for John's gospel in particular it is important that the 'Word' of God is 'made flesh', and that the claims that Jesus makes for himself (such as 'I am the light of the world') are backed up by complementary action. There is a variety in what is said and done as the claims of God's kingdom are pressed home.

If preaching is this proclamation of good news about Jesus Christ, we have to ask whether it is always apparent in our worship. It is tragic if people have joined in the service of the church and have gone away without hearing something positive. Our message may not always make them 'happy', for part of the purpose of the gospel is to confront human sin and seek to face up to the darkness in our life together. But worship ought to offer hope because of the presence of a living Lord. One meeting of local church leaders was convened because the congregation was going through bad times. Literal cracks in the building had revealed serious cracks in the fellowship and had given rise to mistrust and even dislike amongst the members. There was general depression as the meeting progressed. At length the chairman asked: 'Isn't there anything good that we can say about this church?' After a silence, an elderly man replied: 'Well, I suppose that we believe that when we meet on a Sunday morning that Jesus Christ is with us.' That acknowledgement was the turning point on a long and hard road that led to a change of attitude in the congregation, and to subsequent growth. It was the application of 'good news' to the people of God in a particular situation. The life of the Church is dependent on an awareness of the presence of the living Christ, and the preacher's privilege is to open up that truth as the people come together.

James S Stewart drew attention to the five reasons for the victory of Christianity which Gibbon gave in his *Decline and Fall of the Roman Empire*: Christian enthusiasm, belief in immortality, miracles, ethics and organisation. Stewart then asserted that Gibbon 'had left out the one decisive factor: the presence of the proclamation of the living Christ. For what people heard, listening to the apostles, was not simply a human testimony: it was the self-testimony of the risen Jesus. They did not say: "This is the truth: we will learn it, and it will instruct us". They said, "This is the Lord: we have waited for him, and he will save us."'[1] As we engage in the same basic proclamation as the apostles, we are not setting out a set of rules, but asserting our Lord's presence. That fact will necessitate our being alert concerning how best to offer him as a living person to living persons.

The preacher may be ordained and 'full-time', or may be a lay person whose work is spent largely in earning a living as farmer or accountant, nurse or schoolteacher, or as housewife, mother, carer. Part of the variety that the Church needs in the pulpit will be supplied naturally out of the many backgrounds from which the preachers come. It will be well if we make use of our special interests and skills. The more we can be 'ourselves' in the pulpit, the richer will be the contribution to the Church's ministry. This is not an argument for eccentricity, though eccentrics in the pulpit have in fact a fine record of effectiveness. It is to argue that we should duly use the gifts that God has given us and the experiences that he provides in our daily life. The accountant may have something to say about integrity in commercial life, whilst the farmer may speak with some feeling about strained relationships over the use of land or the buying and selling of animals. Someone in a caring profession will have insight into human needs which will enrich what they can tell of God's compassion. There will be for each of them moments when the biblical message has come alive in their particular environment, and they will be able to say, 'This I know!' To share such convictions will help to build up the people of God.

But alongside this natural variety which the preachers provide as a body, there is the variety at which each of us needs to work. We tend to fall into patterns of working, and to some extent they give us strength. But where the congregation can guess what we are going to say and how we are going to say it, we shall be less effective than we ought. If we always have three points, there will be little surprise. If we always preach for half-an-hour, it is an invitation to switch off attention temporarily in the middle. If we always use the same kind of illustrations, there will be a lack of freshness.

We are not seeking variety for its own sake, so as to be able to show that we have the ability to do the same thing in several different ways. Our aim is to discover what is the most appropriate way of preaching in each situation, so that hearers may be helped and God may be glorified. We have already been given a demanding and worthwhile task, as we preach the good news of the kingdom of God. The challenge to find ways of bringing variety into our preaching makes it more stimulating still.

2

VARIETY IN LENGTH

A famous 'name' had come to a meal before preaching at our church. 'How long do you normally preach for?' he asked. 'Twenty minutes,' was the reply. 'Oh, I shall need forty-five. I have three points, and they all need developing.' 'You will have to shorten it,' said his wife. In the event, he did. There were two points, and the sermon lasted thirty minutes. Afterwards, members of the congregation were enthusiastic. 'Why didn't he go on longer? We could have listened for hours.'

Few preachers have the ability to carry along a congregation like that. There needs to be a blending of the skill of the preacher, the quality of the subject matter and the commitment of the hearers to produce enthusiasm for a forty-five minutes sermon. Fortunately, living Christian truth can be expounded in much less than three-quarters of an hour. But part of the preparation of the preacher can usefully be in asking the question 'How long, O Lord?' Those words from the Book of Revelation were originally attributed to the expectant martyrs looking for the consummation of God's kingdom. They can fittingly be appropriated by the preacher who is humbly waiting for a message from the Lord.

The world of athletics can offer an analogy. Runners understandably tend to specialise, but they have a wide range of choices falling basically into four categories. There is the marathon, over twenty-six miles of hard work. There are the long-distance races of 10,000 or 5,000 metres, or the middle-distances of 3,000, 1,500 or 800 metres. There are the 200 and 100 metres sprints, and even a 60 metres 'dash' at indoor events.

Similarly the preacher faces choices about the length of the sermon, and it is at these we shall look. We can again use four categories. There are times for a very long sermon, a 'marathon', which we can set (perhaps arbitrarily) at about forty-five minutes. There is the 'basic' sermon, of about twenty minutes; and there are services where a 'short' sermon of about ten minutes is entirely appropriate. There are also occasions when three minutes is all that is needed, though it must not be a 'sprint' in terms of breathlessly trying to pack too much into a short space.

Unlike the runner, the preacher does not need to specialise. Even the average preacher can expect to turn his or her skills to a breadth of operation which would be quite impracticable for the top-class athlete.

1   '45' - *the long sermon*

There are churches where a forty-five minutes sermon is expected every Sunday, but they are very few and most of us will never be invited to them. However, there are certain times when the '45' is justified, and every preacher needs to be prepared to engage in such a task. One such occasion is the *celebration*, perhaps an evening of joyous worship where people are happy to give time for a lengthy exposition of a biblical theme. Then there is the service where *teaching* on a specific subject is requested of the preacher (perhaps as part of a series, led by several preachers) and where time is needed to do justice to the theme. Thirdly there is the occasion where *circumstances* demand that a worthy presentation can be made about a theme of particular interest or relevance.

To speak at such length needs skill, experience, proper preparation and real discipline. Everyone has sat under the preacher who rambles on, sometimes incoherently, with frequent repetition, seeming to have no real point and no obvious place of conclusion. We need to be aware of such dangers. We need also to understand that a forty-five minutes address is not two twenty minutes sermons stitched together. The patching will show and we shall be seen to be poor workers. The subject needs to be large and worthwhile; there must be a strong framework (going beyond the customary three points if necessary); and there ought to be a balance of lighter material mixed in so that once in a while the concentration of the hearer can relax.

(a) *The Celebration Event* used characteristically to be the Methodist Circuit Rally, which is rare in these days. People came together from a group of churches, enjoyed lively singing as they worshipped, and heard a preacher (usually well-known) who was able to offer an inspiring message. The celebration now is more likely to be an enthusiastic evening with plenty of modern worship songs, led by a number of people with particular gifts. There will be a strong expectation that the sermon will contain good biblical teaching, and that this will be of some considerable length. If the invitation comes to share in such an occasion, the preacher needs to be able to respond appropriately.

James S Stewart of New College, Edinburgh, had a sermon entitled 'Why be a Christian?' which he preached with great effect at an anniversary gathering at the former Methodist Eastbrook Hall in Bradford. The text was Deuteronomy 33:29. It was not expounded in detail. It was more an introduction to the theme, which was to set out the claims for the new life to be found in Christ. It is (i) happier than any other; (ii) harder than any other; (iii) holier than any other; and (iv) more hopeful than any other. Each point was well-argued, and as he closed Dr Stewart added a brief final point: (v) this Christian calling is his (Jesus') life. We are offered Jesus himself.

The points built up, and led to the centrality of Christ. The message came over to the hearers with freshness and conviction. The alliteration with the five h's helped to keep it in the memory. The sermon was just right for such an occasion, reminding the people about the heart of their faith.

The subject may well be chosen for anyone invited to preach at a celebration, but if there is a free choice, it is important to seek to be relevant and encouraging. People who attend celebrations usually want to grow in Christian faith and experience, and there is no shortage of biblical material. Nehemiah 8:10 or Philippians 4:4 are good bases for speaking about joy in the Christian life. Acts 1:8 or 2 Corinthians 12:9 are about the renewing power which the Lord offers, not least to those who are struggling. 1 Corinthians 15:58 gives firm encouragement, based as it is on the fact of the resurrection of Christ. It can speak well to those who put in a great deal of effort to witness in an unresponsive neighbourhood. 2 Peter 3:18 or Colossians 3:12-14 point to patterns of Christian growth. Another important theme could be that of God's greatness in his universe. It will test any preacher who attempts to deal with it, but there is a fascinating translation of Romans 11:36 in the New English Bible, where God is described as being 'Source, Guide and Goal of all that is'. The past, the present and the future are all in his hands.

The aim of the celebration is on the one hand simply to enjoy God (as the Westminster Confession invites us to do), and the fact that we belong to him; and on the other hand to catch a fresh vision of Christ and his work in the world and the church, so as to appropriate anew the strength provided by the Spirit for Christian life and service. The time that the long sermon provides will enable you to quote freely from Christian biography and experience, which are important sources for building up the spiritual life.

(b) A second area where the long sermon may be required is that of *teaching*. Many churches have only a small evening congregation, yet it is usually made up of some of the keenest Christians. They may suggest a series which will teach them more about the faith. It will be a positive contribution to the church's life, and in addition it may prove to be an attraction to those who do not normally attend in the evening. For a subject to be dealt with adequately, more than the customary twenty minutes will doubtless be required. The congregation will be glad to give the preacher more time.

Almost certainly you will be asked to deal with a specific subject which fits into a series. Imagine that you have been requested to look at Christian Baptism. You will have plenty of work to do in looking up the biblical references and in covering as much background reading as you can. It is important not to produce a lecture. There must be sound teaching, as accurate and objective as you are able to make it; but what you say must ultimately be rooted in the experience and needs of the local church. Your task is not to shower people with information, which may send them away confused, but to inform and stimulate their faith.

So you set out to ask questions of yourself. What did Jesus' own baptism mean to him? What commands did he give to the disciples about baptism? What do the accounts of baptism in the Acts of the Apostles have to say to us? How highly does Paul value baptism? What other references are there in the New Testament? Are there any helpful insights in the Old Testament experience of the People of God? Where does the baptism of infants fit in? What has been the teaching of the church about baptism over the centuries? Are there conditions that ought to be laid down about infant baptism? What are the experiences of the local church concerning baptism? To answer the last question you will need to talk with one or two of the local leaders.

How do you place this mass of material that you have gathered before your hearers in an act of worship?

(i) You could circulate the list of questions that you posed for yourself, and report on your findings. As you conclude, you could emphasise the way in which God's grace underlies all that we do in baptism. Martin Luther found it helpful to remind himself: 'I am a baptised man.' God had taken hold of him through this sacrament, and that fact sustained him in difficult times.

(ii) You could take three (or more) points under which you develop your theme: for example (1) Baptism and Jesus; (2) Baptism and the early church; (3) Baptism and our church today.

(iii) You could use the three-points method in a different way, speaking of baptism as a sign of (1) God's grace; (2) people's commitment; (3) the church's mission.

If you can teach well and clearly (and of course that can be done in any length of sermon), there will be those who are fascinated to discover new truth. Some may suggest that they prefer a 'simple faith' (whatever that may be); but whatever the response your aim will have been to build and strengthen faith through the setting out of Christian beliefs.

(c) There are times when *circumstances* demand or give opportunity for a long sermon. One example of such a special occasion was provided by William Sangster when he was minister at Westminster Central Hall. Methodism had earmarked 1953 as a year of evangelism, and on the last Sunday of 1952 he preached on the theme 'What would a Revival of Religion do for Britain?' The sermon was widely reported in the national press on the following day. Sangster had ten points (which could hardly have been dealt with in twenty minutes!): (1) a revival would pay old debts, as it had done in the Welsh revival of the early twentieth century; (2) it would reduce sexual immorality; (3) it would disinfect the theatre and the press; (4) it would cut the divorce rate; (5) it would reduce juvenile crime; (6) it would lessen the prison population; (7) it would improve the quality and increase the output of work; (8) it would restore to the nation a sense of high destiny; (9) it would make us invincible in the war of ideas; and (10) it would give happiness and peace to the people.

When this sermon was subsequently published in pamphlet form, Sangster added a meditation on 2 Chronicles 7:14 as a guide to the way in which revival could come.

This is a good example of Topical preaching, which we shall consider later.[1] The theme of the sermon springs from contemporary circumstances and needs. It is not a piece of biblical exegesis as such, but is heavily dependent on the general theme of the Bible and the characteristics and sense of calling that God offers to and demands from his people.

The revival did not come in that year of evangelism, which may be a reason why the outline of a sermon produced long ago still seems relevant. From the Christian point of view, there is so much that has not changed for the better. But our immediate point is that such a large theme demanded time for adequate development.

Such an opportunity will come rarely, if ever, for most preachers. But there are moments when it is good to stand back and reflect at length on the state of a church. The annual church anniversary or patronal festival is one such, especially if it is a matter of golden jubilee or centenary. To look in some depth at the past, with a prophetic eye to the future, can be of value. John Wesley had a sermon on the words 'What hath God wrought' from Numbers 23:23 in which he reminded his hearers of the way in which Methodism had grown. For us, it is good to have an opportunity to look back, not with nostalgia to the 'good old days', but with gratitude for what God has done; and then to look forward in faith. The longer ending of Mark's gospel (which most scholars take to be a later addition to the place where Mark's work breaks off at 16:8) has a phrase about the Lord 'working with' his disciples and 'confirming' his word. Many a congregation today needs similar encouragement to believe in the activity of Christ amongst them. A written history of the church, if one exists, or memories from some of the older members, are good places to begin such a sermon. With a long sermon there will then be time to set out something of what is happening in the present life of the church, and the steps of faith to be taken to enable even more to be received from God. The church's story is seen in the light of God's purposes.

(2) '20' - *the basic length sermon*

The bishop who was asked by the curate how long he ought to preach for is said to have given the reply: 'About twenty minutes – and about God.' The second piece of advice was an essential; the first piece was probably wise.

Most congregations expect that the sermon will be about twenty minutes in length. One or two preachers may make a modest bid for popularity by cutting down to a quarter of an hour, but there are good reasons for thinking carefully before you do this. On the one hand we have to acknowledge that in our television age it is generally believed that the attention span is only fifteen minutes. (Yet it is worth noting that there are one or two programmes where a single speaker takes up about half-an-hour, without visual effects or being questioned by others. It is presumed that a serious subject will be responded to by keen viewers.) On the other side of the argument is the fact that most churchgoers admit to having very little detailed knowledge about the faith. Apart from the more elderly, few have been brought up on the Bible at home or in Sunday school, and they are aware of their lack when questioned by friends or colleagues. In consequence it is important that the preaching slot each Sunday should be well used so as to build up both individual faith and the life of the church. The extra five minutes may not be too much to request.

If your hearers have a limited attention span, and if you lack the ability to sustain twenty minutes, then be aware of these factors. Fifteen minutes may well then be right; but if this is the case, make sure that the time is well stewarded, with good and solid material being used.

If we return to the analogy of athletics, the 10,000 or 5,000 metres runner has a particular technique to learn. Stamina is needed, as is the craft of pacing oneself throughout the race and responding to the efforts of the other competitors. Similarly there is a good deal to learn about the preaching of this basic length sermon. It requires plenty of relevant material (and there is an art in leaving out what is not relevant); it needs the right mixture of detailed statement of the theme and lighter moments of illustration; and possibly it will contain a moment or two when there is a summing up of the journey so far. There may even be some effort needed to recapture the attention of those who thoughts appear to be wandering.

Just as there is a widespread assumption that a sermon will last about twenty minutes, so in many circles there is the expectation that it will consist of three points. It is easy to dismiss the 'three-decker' sermon as old-fashioned, but it has many values. The preacher has a number of way-marks to keep him or her on the track.

Begin to wander or get lost, and you can soon come back to the main theme. Most points can be adequately expounded in five minutes. Three sections of about five minutes each, plus an introduction and conclusion totalling five minutes, and you have your twenty. As far as the congregation is concerned, if three points are clearly stated (especially if they are set out at the beginning of the sermon) they can sense that progress is being made. They can follow as the sermon develops, and if the points are good they may well remain in the memory afterwards.

But there can be disadvantages, if the making of three points (just because one is searching for three) gives the impression of being artificial. There can be a danger of appearing to make the whole framework of the sermon contrived. The material does not always naturally divide into three, and the preacher needs to use common sense.

However, some texts naturally offer us three points. Micah's classic statement of God's requirements (6:8) talks of living justly, loving mercy and walking humbly in God's presence. One hardly needs to look for a different framework. Similarly, when Jesus describes himself as the true vine (John 15:1-5) he goes on to speak of his Father as the gardener and the privilege which the disciples have of being fruitful branches. Three natural points are there for exposition. Likewise there is the memorable statement about grace, salvation and faith in Ephesians 2:8.

Imagination, carefully used, can create a three-point sermon out of material not obviously falling into three parts. For example, in Luke 1:38 Mary responds to the angel's message by declaring that she is willing to be the Lord's servant. It is possible to speak about her experience and attitude, and to describe Mary as (1) Waiting (she belonged to the quiet, faithful people whom we find in Luke 1-2, waiting for God to work openly once again amongst his people); (2) Wondering (why choose me? how can a thing like this happen?); and (3) Willing (she is shown as happily responding to God's will).

But the preacher must beware of becoming predictable. If there are always three points, it can encourage the congregation to try to out-guess the preacher; but, more importantly, an element of freshness may be lost. If the text or theme does not naturally call for three points, perhaps two, four or even five, are right. Some texts almost demand two points. Jeremiah describes the New Covenant in chapter 31 of his prophecy, and in verse 34 there is the clear statement from the Lord: 'I will forgive their wickedness, and will remember their sins no more.' It is part of God's graciousness in his dealings with us that he forgives – and forgets. Then, in the Revelation of John, as the vision moves to its climax, there is a description of the adoration of the Lord because of his victory over the power of evil which has been rampant in his world. There is a great cry: 'Amen, Hallelujah!' (19:4). Those two words may well represent the response of the Church today for what God has done in Christ: 'So be it! Praise the Lord!' The two points of glad acceptance and joyous adoration say it all.

Similarly there are texts which virtually demand consideration under four headings. The description of life in the earliest Church speaks of the apostles' teaching, fellowship, the breaking of bread and prayer (Acts 2:42). Then in the pastoral prayer in Ephesians 3:18 the quality of God's love is referred to in the four dimensions of breadth, length, height and depth.

Four points in a sermon imply slightly less material under each heading than would be needed for three, just as two points suggest the need for more material. For a twenty minutes sermon it is best not to exceed four points. Even four will demand discipline if the sermon is not to exceed the planned time.

The creation of headings may occur in a number of ways. They may spring directly from the words of the text itself. They may come from an attempt to analyse the context, as with Mary's description of herself as God's servant. They may flow logically from the starting point. Towards the end of his life Paul speaks of John Mark as 'helpful to me in my ministry' (2 Timothy 4:11). Paul had not always seen Mark in that way. The young man of (1) promise (perhaps witness to Jesus' arrest, whose home had been a meeting place for the early church, and who had gone with Paul and Barnabas to Cyprus) had become (2) a failure, whom Paul no longer cared to trust. But now there is (3) restoration, doubtless because Mark's work in the meantime had caused Paul to change his attitude (cf. Mark 14:51; Acts 12:12, 13:5, 13; 15:37-39). The natural progression tells a story of Christian renewal, readily applicable to today's discipleship.[2]

It is justifiable to make use of alliteration in one's points, and it can be valuable if it makes them memorable. Years ago a national newspaper advertised itself as being Readable, Reliable and Realistic. Those words were a gift to a hard-pressed preacher trying to find a good outline for a Bible Sunday sermon. Some have the gift of alliteration or the creation of memorable or balanced phrases for headings.

But there are preachers whose ambitions go beyond their main headings. Alliterated points are each broken into alliterated sub-divisions, which themselves are similarly divided. Unless a preacher has a real gift in this area, he or she must exercise extreme caution. It is well to remember the old advice that the preacher is not there to show how clever he or she is, but how wonderful Jesus is. Alliteration is to be the servant of our memories, not the master of our construction.

As the preacher decides what headings may be most appropriate for the development of the theme, it is important to ask: what is *the* point that this text is making, or that I am wanting to draw out from this passage? A lecture may make many points, as in fact may a sermon. But the sermon seeks to present a Christian truth, or to press home some challenge, and it is well to be as specific as possible. My two, three, four (or even more) points need to be directed to the aim of building up faith and practice. Have I a single aim in mind as I set out to prepare and preach? Is there a strong possibility that at the end of the service the congregation will be clear what that aim was?

One other question may be asked about the twenty minutes sermon. May there not be occasions when it could be fittingly split into two or even three parts and preached at different moments during the service? Whilst the basic aim will be to preach the sermon as a whole, the presence of children throughout an hour's worship may determine that the material (suitably prepared with all ages in mind) should be offered in more manageable slices. Where this is done, great care needs to be given to the framing of the act of worship, lest it become a sandwich of singing hymns with seven minutes addresses in between.

There is an argument for dividing two-point sermons in this way even when only adults are present and the issue is not one of the ability of children to concentrate at length. One of the terrible moments in the Good Friday story is Jesus' cry of dereliction: 'My God, my God, why have you forsaken me?' (Mark 15:34; cf. Matthew 27:46). Those words open a door on the experience of Jesus, virtually beyond our comprehension but referred to by Paul in 2 Corinthians 5:21. There is no way in which we should attempt to water down their meaning. But they are the opening words of Psalm 22, and since according to Luke 23:46 Jesus also quoted Psalm 31:5 whilst on the cross, this psalm was doubtless in his mind. It begins in rejection, but ends in faith. Traditionally scholars have been reluctant to accept that Jesus had the whole psalm in mind; but there are those who believe that he was expressing the real dereliction, yet holding on, as it were, in blind faith. If this were something that you wanted to speak about on Good Friday, there would be the two points, about dereliction and about trust. To move from one to another somewhat abruptly could be inappropriate, whilst to separate them with a hymn, perhaps music and prayer would enable you to paint the picture more sensitively.

(3) '10' - the short sermon

In athletics the classic race was for so long the mile, with the quest as to who would be the first to break the mystic four-minutes barrier. It is now the 1,500 metres, which along with the 3,000 and 800 metres constitute a particular challenge of middle-distance running. There are different techniques needed as compared with long-distance running on the one hand and the sprint races on the other.

For the preacher the ten minutes sermon can be a valuable part of his or her skills. It is not a 'short' sermon in the sense that it is only half a 'real' sermon. It has justification in its own right, and there are times when it is necessary.

For the ordained minister, this length will fit well into many pastoral situations. Some of these may not necessarily affect the lay preacher, but are nevertheless worth reflecting on. There may come a time when you will be asked to help in this way.

There is usually the expectation that an address will be given at a *funeral* service. In the peculiar and time-conscious setting of the crematorium even ten minutes will probably be too much; but if there is a service in church ten minutes will give opportunity to say what is needed about the deceased and about the Christian faith, without becoming an undue burden on sorrowing relatives and friends.

Ten minutes can also be an appropriate length where the main Sunday service includes *Holy Communion* attended by large numbers and where there is the custom of conducting worship in something less than an hour and a quarter. Similarly there are constraints with *all-age worship* where there is a Family or Parade service. Not only may the congregation be hoping that the service will last only an hour (preferably less, with youngsters present): the attention span of younger people will probably be limited unless the preacher has exceptional gifts of communication with them. A brief address earlier in the service with the under-twelves particularly in mind can be followed by a ten-minutes sermon on the same theme. If it is well illustrated the teaching and challenge can be relevant to all ages.

There is also the occasion where a special service of *Christmas carols* provides a feast of worship (if it is properly planned), where the Christian story has been told through Bible readings, and where wisdom will suggest that ten minutes will suffice to bring together the whole celebration and speak of what God has done. To develop the idea of Jesus' 'humbling' himself, as Paul described in Philippians 2, or to consider the grateful praise which was the shepherds' experience in Luke 2:20, can focus the act of worship, and can be achieved within a ten-minutes span.

The short sermon is also relevant where there is a special service relating to a *group or organisation* which is visiting the church for a celebration. There is a church which used to host an annual service for a local ballroom dancing class, and there are many churches which are asked to hold sportsmen's or women's services. A few of the members are likely to be regular churchgoers; most are not. Yet as a group they come willingly. They are not accustomed to long sermons (indeed, any sermons at all), and ten minutes carefully used is probably the right length. It should not be too hard for the visitor to listen, and yet will enable the preacher to say something worthwhile.

There is an art in using the ten minutes which needs to be developed. Whilst we are not cutting down a twenty-minutes sermon, there may be certain similarities in our approach. There may be two or three points (but surely not more?), and illustrations will be needed (but they ought not to be unnecessarily detailed). We need to be as direct as possible, and not waste time.

There is a case for using a ten minutes sermon as an opportunity for telling a story. If we do this it is vital to remind ourselves that we are in the business of communicating biblical truth, and not simply retelling the last story we have heard, however edifying it may appear to be. With a story the details may be important. Story-telling is not the same as using illustrations. It is an ancient art which has been consciously revived in recent years. It lies, of course, at the heart of Jesus' own method of teaching in parables. For the Christian preacher there must be a relevance in the story itself, which will stimulate thought about belief and action as they are found in the New Testament. Further, even though the purpose is to enable reflection, the lessons which the story contains should be fairly clear and unambiguous. One congregation, having been told a story and challenged by the words 'You'll find that there is a lot to think about there!' were quite clear in their reaction. 'We hadn't a clue what he was talking about!' was their claim. Sir Thomas Beecham defined good music as 'that which penetrates the ear with facility and quits the memory with difficulty'. The preacher's aim in telling a story is to enable a picture to be immediately created in the hearer's mind so that it will constantly demand attention as its meaning unfolds.

Another way of using the ten minutes is to base what you say on biographical incidents. The aim is not simply to recount moments from a person's life but to draw out biblical truths from actual experience. For example, John Wesley's Journal for January 1736 contains a graphic and famous account of his voyage to America in the *Simmonds* and the dreadful storm that they endured. Those were the days of small, fragile ships which made the crossing of the Atlantic an extremely risky venture. Wesley was amazed at the calmness of some Germans, men, women and children, who went on praising God whilst the English were terrified. Such faith and peace were unknown to him. It is instructive to compare that incident with an equally well-known story in the Journal, dated October 1743. Wesley was faced at Wednesbury in the West Midlands by a riotous mob out for his blood. He overcame the anger of his opponents and emerged safely from the volatile episode. Telling (without undue detail) these accounts together can lead to considering what Paul claims for the Christian in Colossians 1:11, which the New English Bible translates as 'may he strengthen you . . . with ample power to meet whatever comes with fortitude, patience and joy.' The faith which Wesley had discovered at Aldersgate Street in May 1738 between those two events had made all the difference to the way in which he was able to face the most demanding circumstances. Two points, neatly balanced or contrasted, and pointing to Bible truth or experience, can be a good pattern for this length of sermon.

But you will not always need to turn to the past for such illustrative experiences. It should not be difficult to find a recent incident that may already be in your listeners' minds and which will gain from being seen in the light of the Bible.

A number of radio speakers offer a model of how to use ten minutes or so. There are many examples where a subject, serious or amusing, is developed within this limit. Points may not be made, as a preacher might, but there is usually a progression from an arresting beginning to a worthwhile (and probably thought-provoking) conclusion. For the sake of the gospel, we may well covet something of the ability to interest, hold, inform and challenge.

(4) '3' - the brief sermon

There is an honourable place in the athletics world for the sprint. The 100 and 200 metres races draw attention because of the stars who run in them. An indoor event may include the 60 metres race, over almost as soon as it has begun. Concluding our use of the analogy, there is an important place for the 'brief' sermon which lasts only about three minutes.

This ought not to be seen as an 'apology' for a sermon, but something having its own value. One congregation was just settling to listen to a visiting dignitary when suddenly he concluded. What he said was useful as an introduction to a sermon, but took his hearers nowhere. However, given the right preparation, it is possible to preach 'briefly' to real effect.

We have already considered the way in which a ten minutes sermon can be preached at a funeral or communion service. In fact the brief sermon may sometimes be needed instead. The *funeral* or thanksgiving service conducted within the time restriction of a crematorium may give opportunity only for three minutes; or it may be that the extreme distress of the mourners in certain circumstances calls for such brevity. There are often mid-week celebrations of *Holy Communion* where time is of the essence: people may be on their way to work, or worshipping during a lunch-break. There are those who argue that the sacrament ought always to be accompanied by the preaching of the Word; and there can be enrichment provided by even a brief exposition. *Infant baptism* is sometimes celebrated outside the main worship of the church, perhaps because the family and friends are not regular churchgoers. In such cases an opportunity to speak of God's grace and our response ought not to be missed; but neither baby nor family is likely to appreciate a full-scale sermon. Three minutes can offer the chance to expound some aspect of the sacrament.

The lay preacher is often called on to make a brief contribution in a service of worship which he or she does not happen to be leading. Perhaps two or three people are looking at some aspect of the theme of the service. To be able to use three minutes well is a real gift, and will help in guiding others asked to speak in similar circumstances.

Depending on the rate at which the preacher speaks, the three minutes sermon presupposes something between four and five hundred words. This may seem a simple task; perhaps it is. The boredom factor will hardly raise its head in so short a time. Yet it is possible to say nothing in three minutes, and constructive use of this time is a skill that needs to be learned and constantly polished. It is said that President F D Roosevelt was ready to address the American nation virtually at the drop of a hat; but if he had to give a three minutes talk on an important issue (those were the days of radio only) he needed three weeks' notice. That is doubtless an exaggeration, yet it does point to the need to decide clearly what is to be said, and then to say it directly, without waste of words.

Our pattern here is once again the radio or television reporter who has limited time in which to present facts and perhaps to make a brief comment. The memorable phrase or two may help. Attention must be captured immediately, every word must count, facts or events must be carefully marshalled. The report must not peter out, but conclude firmly. The listener or viewer gains the impression of competent reporting and feels that he or she now understands something of what has been talked about.

That will be the preacher's aim too, in this brief address. Basically there will be one theme, which may revolve around a picture or illustration, a graphic phrase from the Bible, or an incident from national or local life. A strong opening will lead to that theme, which is then related to biblical truth, and have a firm closing sentence.

For example, at a funeral one could quote Susannah Wesley's words just before she died: 'Children, as soon as I am released, sing a psalm of praise to God.' Those words capture her strong belief in a God who would give her even greater life beyond death, and were an encouragement to her children not to be broken by grief but to be thankful for all that their mother had meant to them. She was acknowledging the truth that Paul expressed, that nothing in life or in death can separate us from God's love as we experience it in Jesus Christ (Romans 8:38-39). Susannah's words, the biblical conviction, and a brief word of application to the family and friends could all be contained to good effect within three minutes.

Or there is the moving example of the young couple, tragically losing a small child, whose faith was such that they said that they were determined not to have the experience without discovering the meaning. Only they could engage on that quest, although family and friends could stand by; but such faith and courage in darkness, together with Paul's words from Romans 8, could be used sensitively so as to undergird faith for others in similar trouble.

✯ ✯ ✯ ✯ ✯

John Ruskin spoke about preaching as 'thirty minutes to raise the dead in'. He was speaking within his own context of the nineteenth century: perhaps the half-hour was customary, and perhaps the churchgoers were likely to be spiritually dead. We can adjust his thirty minutes to suit our circumstances: there is nothing sacrosanct about any length of time for a sermon. But Ruskin does challenge us to have a similar dynamic expectation when we preach, however long we may take. What we say is not to be offered in a take-it-or-leave-it manner. There are people listening who struggle with doubt or with concern for loved ones. Others are under genuine stress, at home or at work. They are eager to know more about how they can love and serve Christ, and receive what he has to offer. Believe in your message, and discover the best framework in which to offer it.

3

VARIETY IN APPROACH

There was a preacher who was said to have a hundred texts but only one sermon. Wherever he started, the material was the same. No doubt that story was apocryphal, but we can heed the warning. In his defence, it could be claimed that it is not our purpose to say anything new: the gospel comes handed down to us over the generations. But in fact we have a responsibility to offer the good news with freshness and relevance, and to understand that there are many things that the Bible has to say to us. Churning out the same old words and ideas is not acceptable.

There are basically three ways in which we can approach the making of a sermon.

(1) The sermon may be *Expository*; that is, it will seek to open up a word, phrase or longer biblical passage.

(2) The sermon may be *Topical*; that is, it will emerge from some event or issue which is demanding attention at the time, whether at local, national or international level.

(3) The sermon may be *Experiential*; that is, it will arise from a subject in the experience of the preacher or congregation, or from a wider context.

(1) Expository Preaching

A dictionary will speak of 'expository' as something which gives an explanatory account. When we engage in expository preaching we are seeking to explain the meaning of a particular passage in the Bible. We set it in the context of the whole of human knowledge, and as we do so we believe that the Bible opens up for us insight into the nature of humanity and its purpose on this planet. Our task is to clarify as far as possible those insights for people who face the joys and sorrows of contemporary living. Whatever may be the way in which as individuals we understand the authority of the Bible, this is the book whose message we proclaim.

As we prepare to offer exposition of the biblical text, there are two other words which we need to bear in mind. One is *Exegesis,* which also is usually defined in terms of explanation. In fact, it lies behind exposition, for exegesis is the explaining (insofar as we are able) of what the original text meant, so that we may go on to the expository task, which is the explaining of what that text may, or should, mean in our own day. Behind all this is the science of *Hermeneutics,* which has to do with the general rules of interpretation of the Bible. Do I take this passage literally, or is it to be understood in figurative terms only? For most of us the story of the Good Samaritan (in Luke 10) is fairly straightforward, culminating in a trenchant challenge to 'do likewise'. But St Augustine had a famous interpretation which transformed that story into an allegory where every detail counted. So, for example, the two pence given to the innkeeper came to stand for two sacraments. Such matters are the basic questions with which hermeneutics deal. They should be in the back of our minds as we turn to the preparation of a sermon.

So when we approach a text with the eye of an expositor, we have to ask three classic questions:
    (i) What did the biblical writer mean when he wrote these words (given the world in which he lived)?
    (ii) What did his readers understand when they read these words? (We may hope that the two answers so far are in agreement, but that may not in fact be the case.)

(iii) What do these words mean to us, living in a very different world but within the same overarching grace of God's purposes?

But what do we actually preach about? How do we begin to decide what piece of the Bible to expound? This brings us to the question of the use of *the lectionary* which many churches now provide. There was a time in Methodism when the same lectionary readings came round in a two-yearly cycle, with the same theme given for most of the Sundays each year. There was justifiable anxiety about frequent repetition of a limited number of themes. With the present lectionary in *The Methodist Worship Book* the material is much more varied, there is choice within a given Sunday, and set themes are not presented. So for those who had reservations in the past, many of the weaknesses have been remedied. One major argument for the use of a good lectionary is continuity in the reading of the Bible, which is of considerable educational value for any congregation.

But if one follows the lectionary, how is the material to be used? There are at least four possibilities.

(i) You can select one *main lesson*, and use the others as illustrative material for your subject.
(ii) You can find a *theme* which knits together the lessons you have chosen. (A hint for that theme may sometimes be found in the Collect for the day.)
(iii) You can choose a *text* that strikes you from one of the lessons, and base your sermon on that, reading whatever other lessons seem most appropriate.
(iv) You can assess whether there is any *subject* that you would like to pursue, where the lessons are those which are 'related'. This is somewhat similar to seeking a theme, as in (ii), but stems from the passages in the Revised Common Lectionary. During many of the Sundays of Ordinary Time, the lectionary offers either 'continuous' readings (where the Old Testament passage is part of a series), or 'related' (where the Old Testament passage is linked with the Gospel). We shall take

note of this possibility in our fourth example, which is from the 21st Sunday in Ordinary Time (Year A).[1]

We can look at some examples.

(a) The *4th Sunday in Ordinary Time* in *Year A* of the lectionary contains the following readings:

>   Micah 6:1-8
>   Psalm 15
>   1 Corinthians 1:18-31
>   Matthew 5:1-12

(i) If you take the Micah passage as the *main lesson*, you can expound verse 8, the great requirements of the Lord. The verse clearly suggests a three point sermon, and it is useful to realise that the other lessons for the day neatly fit into an exposition. We are to:

  (1) *do justly* – and Psalm 15 gives an account of what 'upright' dealing meant for the people of the Old Testament;

  (2) *love mercy* – and Matthew 5:1-12 (the beginning of the Sermon on the Mount) exemplifies this alternative lifestyle that Jesus both demands and offers; and

  (3) *walk humbly* with God. 1 Corinthians 1 has a famous description of the boastfulness of human life, which is set against the proper humility of the believer before Christ and his cross.

(ii) You could state the overall *theme* of these readings as being God's requirement of men and women (as set out in Micah). Three points could be:

  (1) *humility* and just dealing (as in Micah and the psalm);

  (2) *commitment* to the alternative lifestyle of the kingdom of God (as in Matthew 5);

  (3) *response* in faith to the grace of God in Christ (as Paul set out in 1 Corinthians 1).

(iii) There is a wide freedom to choose a *text* from these passages. If you took 1 Corinthians 1:18, the message of the cross can be seen as telling us:
- (1) what *God* is like (righteous, humble and self-giving);
- (2) what *human nature* can be like – when 'wisdom' and 'power' mislead us;
- (3) what *Christian living* can be like – the context talks about true wisdom, salvation and consecration.

(b) The *Easter day* readings in *Year A* include:
Acts 10:34-43
Psalm 118:1-2, 14-24
Colossians 3:1-4
John 20:1-18

(i) As a *main lesson,* John 20:1-18 speaks of the empty tomb and the appearance to Mary. We are invited to see that (1) Christ has conquered death, and (2) is available to his disciples. The other readings reinforce these two great claims. Psalm 118:24 tells us that God is at work in his world; that was the experience of his people, the Jews. Acts 10 records the preaching of the early Church, and the way in which the cross and resurrection were at the heart of the message as the believers spoke about Jesus. In the Colossians reading we see the way in which the Church has the privilege of knowing the risen Christ and sharing his life (and love and joy, if one looks on through the chapter). Our experience of life in the Church ought to be a major proof of the fact that Christ has risen.

(ii) As an overall *theme* one very obvious title could be 'Christ is alive!' The material lends itself to use as follows:
- (1) *Realising* that Jesus is alive (John 20).
- (2) *Reporting* the gospel story (Acts 10).

>   (3) *Recognising* Jesus in the life of the church (Colossians 3).
>
> (iii) The *text* could be Colossians 3:1 – Risen with Christ. The experience of the early Church was:
>
>   (1) based on the facts of *Jesus' ministry* in Acts 10: the kingdom of God was let loose in his coming;
>
>   (2) based on the facts of John 20: *the empty tomb and the appearances;*
>
>   (3) based on the kind of things that happened in *the church at Colossae:* Christians found themselves drawn together in love.

The material in each approach is basically the same, but is presented with different emphases. For some preachers there is no difficulty in believing in an empty tomb: they have looked at the biblical evidence and are able to accept its validity. They may feel it right to comment on this. Others may not be able to preach with such conviction on the matter. They will need to explain how it is that they nevertheless share in the Easter faith.

(c) The *Pentecost* readings in *Year B* include:

> Acts 2:1-21
> Psalm 104:24-34, 35b
> Romans 8:22-27
> John 15:26-27; 16:4b-15

> (i) The *main lesson* could be Acts 2:1-21, which could be used to explore the subject 'The birth of the Church'. Through the coming of the Spirit, God
>
>   (1) makes new *people* (these 'failed' disciples become effective witnesses);
>
>   (2) makes a new *community* (as the latter part of the chapter shows);
>
>   (3) makes a new *creation* (as people of different nations come to share in the grace of God).

(ii) An overall *theme* would be to use the material to speak of God's gift of the Spirit, somewhat similarly to what we have already described:
  (1) the *Promise* of the Spirit (John 15-16);
  (2) the *Coming* of the Spirit (Acts 2);
  (3) the *Privilege* of the Christian in sharing in the life of the Spirit (Romans 8).

(iii) The *text* could be Acts 2:4, dealing with the filling of the disciples' lives with the Spirit. Some of the consequences of this were:
  (1) an ability to *communicate* the gospel;
  (2) a *commitment* to discipleship in a new way;
  (3) the development of a *community* of believers;
  (4) the *changing* of lives and attitudes.

These points are to be found as chapter 2 develops.

(d) The 21st Sunday in Ordinary Time in Year A has the following:[2]

For the 'continuous' readings –
  Exodus 1:8-2:10
  Psalm 124
  Romans 12:1-8
  Matthew 16:13-20

For the 'related' readings –
  Isaiah 51:1-6
  Psalm 138
  Romans 12:1-8
  Matthew 16:13-20

There are two collects suggested for the day, the first of which contains the themes of freedom and justice and which is therefore related to the Exodus reading in the 'continuous' lection:

  Holy God,
  You liberate the oppressed and make a way of
    salvation.

Unite us with all who cry for justice,
And lead us together into freedom;
Through our Lord and Liberator, Jesus Christ.

The second collect relates to the calling together of the people of God, to its unity and its mission:

Merciful God,
Grant that your Church,
Being gathered by your Holy Spirit into one,
May reveal your glory among all peoples,
To the honour of your name;
Through Jesus Christ our Lord.

Here there is reference to the 'related' lection and the Isaiah reading.

(i) If we take the Exodus passage from the 'continuous' reading as our *main lesson*, we are dealing with how God is aware of his people's needs and comes to their help through the provision of Moses as a leader. In the Moses story we see ordinary people, such as the midwives and Moses' sister and mother, bravely confronting the injustice of Egyptian rule. They are apparently insignificant, but they have their part to play in God's plan for freedom for his people. In our own day we need courage to confront injustice, and faith to believe that a series of small actions by ordinary people can be effective as part of God's purpose. The other lessons provide links with this subject. Psalm 124 tells of God's actions for his people; Matthew 16 tells of the choice of Peter; and Romans 12 set out a new life in Christ which is concerned with service and forgiveness.

(ii) There is an overall *theme* in the 'continuous' lessons of God's choice of people, of Moses, or Peter and of ourselves (as we respond to the challenge of Romans 12). Each person serves in a different setting, with differing gifts; but the task for each is to allow God to effect his overall plans through our discipleship.

(iii) There is a wide choice of significant *texts* in these readings. Romans 12:2 makes the contrast of two possible ways of living:

(1) of being *conformed* to one's environment (that is, being squeezed into the mould accepted by most other people); or

(2) of being *transformed* by the inner working of God's Spirit (about which Paul has already been speaking in this letter). Moses and Peter are good examples of those who moved from conforming to being transformed. They were under the Lord's protection (as claimed by Psalm 124). The richness of Romans 12 offers a number of ways to illustrate what transformation means in practical terms.

(iv) For this Sunday we have the alternative of the 'related' readings, and you have the option of looking here for a *subject* to expound. We have seen that the second collect for the day points to the way in which God calls together a people for himself, the unity of that people, and its mission within God's world. Its foundation, as Matthew 16 makes clear, is now the confession of faith in Jesus Christ, and Romans 12 shows something of the expression of its life and service. The new factor in the 'related' readings comes with the passage from Isaiah 51. The 'bedrock' from which Christians are taken is Abraham, who learned to live by faith, obediently following the will of God, sometimes under great difficulty. The prophet offers this comfort of inheriting the promises of Abraham to the dispirited Jews in exile in Babylon. They have to look back to their great heritage, and forward to their great deliverance. Psalm 138 emphasises the greatness of God, and his determination to fulfil his purposes for his people (verse 8). So the import of these passages can suggest a subject for a sermon. God chooses people (our local congregation!) to be his people. He will sustain them as they live by faith; and they have the assurance that his purposes will not fail. This is not triumphalism on our part, nor is it superficiality. It is a matter of placing ourselves within the great sweep of the Bible story.

Our study of these four Sundays has indicated something of the way in which the expository preacher needs to work. Confronted by the biblical texts, I need to do all that is possible to understand them, learning about them and trying to get the 'feel' of what they are saying. Commentaries will be essential reading, and this is why the preacher needs to gather as good a collection as possible of Bible commentaries and background books. As I begin to get the feel of the material, I look for links with today's world, perhaps on matters of principle, perhaps illustrative. Then comes the task of shaping the material that I have gathered. What points ought to be made? Gradually the sermon will be formed.

It is not obligatory to use the lectionary. There are many preachers who are uncomfortable with set readings, feeling that they may be restricted in their freedom to preach on a theme which they believe the Lord has given them. There are dangers in this approach, for we may not be as directly led by God as we think. Further, where we preach often to the same congregation, the people may sense that our choice of themes reflects too much our personal interests. Yet it is important to be ready to yield to the prompting of the Spirit as and when he speaks. It may seem as if something will not leave our mind, or a burden has been laid on our heart. If there is a compulsion to use a certain text, or we are drawn to a particular theme, then we should feel free to respond. If this is a matter of prayer, the Lord will guide and use the work.

Where we accept the freedom to operate in this manner, expository preaching can be employed in a number of ways. For example:

(a) a single *verse or phrase* can be used;

(b) a *longer passage*, up to a chapter in length, can be taken and expounded;

(c) a *whole book* can be preached on. It may be feasible to deal with one of the shorter prophets, say Habakkuk or Haggai, on a single occasion; but in practice a longer book, such as the gospel of Mark, is best looked at chapter by chapter, as in method (b);

(d) *Bible themes* may be followed.

(a) Where a single *verse or phrase* is expounded, there is the opportunity of dealing with it in some depth. It should go without saying that the subject needs to be worthwhile in its own right and relevant to today's needs. Fortunately the preacher nowadays is less tempted to deal with some obscure issue or arcane theological point than were some preachers of previous generations. The material needs to relate both to the nature of the gospel and the lives of the hearers. The themes need to be varied, and it is not a bad thing to invite people from time to time to suggest texts or subjects which they would welcome hearing about.

(b) To take and expound a *longer passage,* up to about a chapter in length, can be beneficial, especially where people have not yet learned to see the Bible as a whole. For many it is a volume of isolated texts or brief devotional readings. Once again the preacher must do a great deal of background work, in order to get the feel of the Bible situation, the shape of the passage and the way in which the writer wanted its argument to flow. We need to concentrate on getting an outline which does justice to the material and which is accessible to the hearer. We need also some insight into how the principles we are discovering relate to present experience.

For example, *Psalm 84* can be seen as expressing the joy that God's house may bring to the worshipper. The writer comes as a pilgrim to the temple in Jerusalem, and discovers (1) joy at the sight of God's house; (2) security as he reflects on the birds nesting there (which would hardly be a cause of celebration for any modern church property steward); (3) renewal, as he thinks of the perils of journeying through desert places, but realises that the Lord provides water in even the most unlikely spots; and (4) grace, as he thinks of the acceptance so freely given by God. (The older translations of verse 10 talk about being a 'doorkeeper' in God's house; but the Revised English Bible captures something of the grace offered to us when it says 'better to linger by the threshold of God's house . . .' We are being encouraged to 'loiter with intent'). At the end of such an exposition (or point by point as the sermon proceeds) it is appropriate to apply these biblical convictions to current life.

Again, Paul's description of Christian living in *Romans 8* speaks of the way in which the Holy Spirit lifts life to a new dimension. The background needs to be stated: Romans 1-7 talks of humankind's need and inability to change itself, and of the gracious intervention of God in Christ: 'God has poured out his love into our hearts by the Holy Spirit, whom he has given us' (5:5). There are four ways mentioned in chapter 8 in which the Spirit works in us. (1) He enables us to have faith (verse 9. This is more explicitly stated in 1 Corinthians 12:3). (2) He guides us in our living (verse 14). (3) He enables us to be sure about our faith: we are God's children (verse 16). (4) He gives us strength in our weakness (verse 26). How does this apply to difficult personal relationships, or to the way we deal with stress or cope with burdens? Knowing a little of the congregation as well as the Bible, the preacher can attempt to make the application. Such a large theme ought to inspire genuine encouragement.

(c) A *whole book* may be used as the basis for exposition. Where a book is short, it may be covered in one sermon, but larger books will need to be dealt with in serial fashion.

The minister who is in the same pulpit regularly will have considerable opportunity to develop a series, whereas the average lay preacher will not. However, many churches welcome series of sermons, and these can be enriched where several people share in them. So there is scope for the lay preacher to join other colleagues, ministerial and lay, to co-operate. It will mean a good deal of detailed planning, but this will bring its own reward.

The *lectionary* is obviously able to be used for a series where consecutive readings from a book are being offered. It is also worthwhile looking in one or two *commentaries* to see whether they provide a useful analysis of the book you have in mind. This may be helpful in highlighting a clear development of the argument of the author, or a number of key themes which may be of value. Some books, however, do not have a clear outline. For example, *Proverbs* is a compendium of 'wise' sayings, some only loosely or not at all connected. In such a case you may need to select say three or four sayings to look at in some depth, in the hope that you may whet the congregation's appetite to do some further browsing. Or you could turn to the Lion Bible Handbook,[3] which suggests five themes from Proverbs 10-31:

(1) The wise person and the fool
(2) The righteous and the wicked
(3) Words and the tongue
(4) The family
(5) Laziness and hard work

The third theme may lead you to the book of James and to Jesus' demands in Matthew 5:33-37. The fourth may lead you to what Paul has to say about this area of discipleship.

The prophet *Haggai* is a useful example of a fairly straightforward message given in two chapters, which can be expounded and applied to today in twenty minutes or half-an-hour. Resist the danger of giving a lecture. But feel able to paint with broad strokes the situation in the sixth century before Christ. The people's hopes had been shattered by exile to Babylon, but whilst there they had been able to grasp the thought of a God who rules over all the nations. Babylon's fall to Cyrus of Persia had enabled some to return home to Jerusalem. There they were faced with the difficult task of rebuilding their life and community. Haggai suggests that they were coping well, with comfortable houses; but he raises the question of priorities. Their experience is that income falls short of requirements (1:6), and he challenges them to make the Lord their priority. The outward sign of this is the rebuilding of the temple. Haggai believes that life will then take on a new meaning, and he goes on to share something of a messianic vision of life under the ruler Zerubbabel.

The picture which Haggai paints is not without its modern parallels, and leads to the question of what ought to be the priorities for Christian people (and indeed any nation) today. How do *we* best bring pleasure to God and honour him (Haggai 1:8)? Probably not in the building of yet more places of worship, but certainly in seeking to see through the lures of immediate gratification and economic pragmatism, to a society where the priorities are related to the justice that God desires. The detail of the priority will vary from congregation to congregation, but the thrust of Haggai's theology should be a stimulus to thought and action.

Few books can be dealt with as succinctly as Haggai, and the exposition of most will need a number of weeks. Part of the art of our task is to shape the series so that it is not so brief as to be unworthy of the material, or so long as to become tedious. There is on record the account of a minister who on arrival at a church announced that he would be preaching his way through Paul's letter to the Philippians. He died quite suddenly, just under two years later, when he was still on chapter 2. The comment was that the congregation was deeply saddened to lose a much-loved minister, but relieved to have a rest from Philippians. A series must not be extended unduly.

Thus *Mark's gospel* could be dealt with in say sixteen weeks, a chapter at a time, and still keep its freshness, if we can find a comprehensive theme that will carry the attention of the listeners. Themes such as Discipleship in Mark's gospel, or the Kingdom of God in Mark's gospel, enable you to go through the material, using selected passages in each chapter to sustain the theme. An alternative approach would be to deal much more briefly with a book, in perhaps three or four sessions, and set out its salient points. For example, the emphases of *Luke's gospel* are well-known, but bear repetition and fresh exposition. They include prayer, Jesus' concern for women, the Holy Spirit, the poor, and the universality of God's grace. These all have something to say to today's Church. You are not offering a detailed commentary, covering every verse in the book. Rather, you are taking specific phrases, passages or incidents and showing how they light up God's activity and our response.

A short series on the *Psalms* can provide an outline of the spiritual life. A few selected psalms offer a framework which can be filled out by reference to the rich vein of New Testament material and Christian biography. For example, the psalms lead us into the world of:

（1）Praise: 96
（2）Prayer: 42
（3）Penitence and Pardon: 51
（4）Peace and Trust: 121
（5）Power to serve the living God: 27

You will have your own favourites under such headings, and so be able to use these old songs to help form a modest handbook for daily life.

Another worthwhile area could be to look in some detail at the life of the early Church as we read about it in *1 Corinthians*, with all the joys and struggles alluded to there. The church was faced with a wide range of problems, some of them raised in correspondence with Paul, others reported to him by Chloe's people. The list is not pleasant: divisions over leadership and social status, litigation, sexual immorality, divorce, freedom to do as one wished even if it harmed fellow-believers, detail about worship and the question of the resurrection of Jesus and its interpretation.

The church members were a very mixed group. Some were wealthy, and could open their homes for worship and fellowship. Others were poor, perhaps employed in the docks, whilst others were slaves, attracted by the Christian message of freedom. Some slaves would be well-educated, and might be tempted to look down on everyone else. How did these people react to the problems they faced as a church? Were they willing to listen to Paul? Had he clear answers to each difficulty? How significant was his emphasis on Christian love so movingly set out in chapter 13?

One way of developing a series on 1 Corinthians could be to go through the 'problems', perhaps two or three each week, and relate them to Paul's assurance of the presence of the living Christ (chapter 15) and the call to Christian love. Where problems are not 'solved', this is the attitude in which Christians seek to face them together. Another way could be to expound the issues in the first week (although this could perhaps depress and even overwhelm the average congregation), the types of people who made up the body of Christ in the second, and to round off in the third week by indicating the spirit of love to which Paul points. This approach could be allied with midweek fellowship groups (if they exist), who could consider (1) what problems do we face as a church? (2) what kinds of people are we within our congregation? And (3) where, in the light of this, are we being led as the body of Christ? Linking the sermon themes with fellowship groups ought to help to 'earth' the studies. The aim of such a study of 1 Corinthians, in the light of the resurrection of Christ and the centrality of love in our discipleship, is the sharing of Paul's conviction in 1 Corinthians 15:58.

What we find in 1 Corinthians provides an example of the difficulty that the expositor will sometimes face, and which ought not to be ignored if we are to retain our integrity. Chapter 14 contains the command that women should be silent in church (verse 34). You may find no difficulty with that verse, but you ought to acknowledge that many people do find it unacceptable. It may be that they in fact hold a very high view of the Bible's authority, but they want to place this command in its appropriate first-century setting in Corinth, and draw a different conclusion for its meaning today. You must not ignore the awkward teaching. If you are aware that you are unclear about a particular issue, and the exposition demands that you deal with it, acknowledge your struggles. Your honesty will be respected, and there may even be someone present who can help you forward in your understanding.

(d) Another way of engaging in expository preaching is to follow a series of *Bible themes*. This may be on a theological issue, or otherwise. You are not tied to one book, but can cover the whole Bible, if necessary. God's grace, his creative purposes, the life of prayer, the demands of discipleship, immediately spring to mind; but a Bible dictionary or handbook will supply many lines of thought.

You will need to give considerable thought to the theme that you have chosen. You will gather references from throughout the Bible; but it is not then a matter of putting them all into a bag, shaking them up, and seeing what comes out. F F Bruce spoke of 'recurring patterns of divine action and human response'.[4] A large part of your task is to trace these accurately. You will expect that references to the grace and mercy of God in the gospels will reveal far more about his nature than could have been appreciated by those who were living in the days of the Books of Kings. We believe that the Old Testament is to be seen in the light of Jesus, so expect to find development within your theme. As you speak about this, it will be both fascinating and helpful to your congregation.

James Black offered a list of ways in which we may set out to expound themes in the Bible. Although somewhat dated, it is worth studying for the way in which it can enable us to compile our own lists. Black set out a number of ways in which we may approach the task:

(1) by problems – as in the Corinthian letters
(2) by vices – as in the book of Amos
(3) by leading ideas (such as we have suggested regarding Luke's gospel)
(4) by events – e.g. the cities in Acts
(5) by portraits
(6) by customs and institutions (here Black turns to Deuteronomy and Numbers with their themes of hospitality, cities of refuge, provision for the poor, the rites of gleaners, harvest laws and the stranger within the gates)
(7) 'crossroads' moments in Jesus' ministry

(8) links and advances in the thinking of Paul. [5]

As you engage in the exposition of the Bible, it is good to keep asking if there are any clear parallels in the life of God's people today. If there are, detail them and illustrate the truths they exemplify. If there appear to be no close parallels, it may still be possible to ask what questions this material should raise for us.

(2) Topical preaching

Topical preaching seeks to address the Christian message to current issues and concerns of immediate relevance to the hearers. In an age when the Bible is little-known, even amongst some churchgoers, it is argued that we do better to start 'where people are' rather than where we may assume or hope their thoughts to be. The world of Haggai is a long way off, quite different from ours, it is suggested; and even the teaching in the gospels may not appear to have much relevance. The worshipper comes to church on Sunday with other things in mind. Television news tells of wars and rumours of wars, of terrible human suffering, and of natural disasters and the impending danger of global warming. Nearer home are worries about stability at work, family tensions and the necessity of balancing the family budget. Start in these areas, rather than the Bible, it is claimed, and you have a better chance of being listened to with some degree of enthusiasm.

This approach to preaching has enjoyed some popularity, not least in the United States of America. In Britain it has a cousin in the BBC's *Thought for the Day*. With only four minutes, the speaker has to grasp immediate attention, deal interestingly with a subject which is probably in the news, and offer some kind of insight. May this not offer a pattern for what we do in the pulpit?

There are a number of cautionary points to make.

(i) There can be value in considering topical matters in this way, but there is a danger in attempting to offer a Christian 'angle' on any and every subject. Most issues are so complex that the preacher will invite ridicule if it is supposed that week after week a subject can be identified and considered in twenty minutes with analysis and comment, as if to say, 'Now we have dealt with that. We will deal with something else next week.' However genuine the approach may be, there is a danger of appearing to be superficial.

(ii) There is the possibility that the congregation may actually be glad to come to church to put aside topical issues for an hour or so. That is *not* to say that they come to engage in a piece of weekly escapism. But having been satiated with secular issues through television and the newspapers, and having tried to take a responsible interest, there is a sense in which they come to worship to change the focus. The purpose is to see God, to sense a little of his majesty and love, and to hear something of what the Bible has to say about human life. It is worth noting that most congregations lose patience with what they call 'political preachers'. They may in fact agree with the points that are being made, but they feel that there is a wider theological dimension which is not being sufficiently considered.

(iii) There is the fact that the preacher is not an expert on topical issues. My analysis of current affairs will be sadly lacking when compared with that of the television correspondent; and my attempt to deal with some medical or scientific issue may appal the genuine expert sitting in the pew. Even an attempt to deal with a personal problem may invite the unspoken comment: 'But you really don't understand *my* situation.' My duty as a preacher may be to comment on large subjects from time to time, but not to presume to expound them in depth.

(iv) In an attempt to be relevant, we may inadvertently give rise to disillusionment. Few of us would claim that the Bible has a clear and instant 'answer' to every problem. We know its value in its revelation of the nature of God and the possibility of the transformation of human life, but that is not to say that as we identify the question we can look up the answer 'in the back of the book'. For some there will be a feeling of being let down if we start with a 'problem' and fail to supply a comprehensive answer.

Topical preaching may in fact be a misnomer. It may indicate the place where one starts, rather than be a matter for detailed consideration in its own right. Our belief as Christians is that our faith is utterly relevant to the world as we find it. We may have as goal a kingdom which lies beyond this life, but in no way is that kingdom world-denying. Indeed, its characteristics as we understand them are a constant challenge to the way in which we act in the present. So there is a sense in which we ought constantly to be aware of topical issues as we preach, but to see them in the light of what the Bible says. Whilst only rarely can we say, 'Here is the answer', there will almost inevitably be insights which provide new understanding and fresh ways forward. The work of the preacher is to consider the issue and then move to exposition about the good news of the kingdom.

War and violence are part of our daily news, so that no longer are they subjects kept for Remembrance Sunday only. Hopes that wars could be fought so that no future generation need engage in conflict have been cruelly dashed. Where is God in all this suffering? Does he care about the kind of people he has made, and about the innocent suffering that inevitably accompanies conflict? What can the preacher say? There is a great deal of violence described in the Old Testament, some of it done in the name of the people of God. But there is a moment in Psalm 46:9 where it is claimed that God 'makes wars cease'. Conflict is not his will, but rather peace and wholesomeness. That was the message of the prophets, but they pointed also to human sin which marred God's plan for his world. Jesus is realistic. He knows the nature of humankind, and says that wars will continue (as in Mark 13). But he calls his followers to be people of peace (Matthew 5:9), and to share in a new lifestyle of forgiveness and love. A changed world can occur only as people voluntarily and genuinely accept the ways of God's kingdom.

The point is that what began as a topical concern over the latest outbreak of violence has led to a consideration of theological issues set out in the Bible. The topic has led to exposition. This is what happened in William Sangster's sermon on Revival that we considered in chapter 2.

Perhaps the key factor in topical preaching is to remember that we are not competent to give a definitive lecture, and that even if we were competent that would not necessarily be our task. We are using a particular way of preaching to relate our faith to everyday affairs. The themes are dominant at the time when we preach, and we take them seriously, but we are relating them to a *person*. We live in God's world, and we bring what we know of the life and teaching of Jesus Christ, together with our awareness of the activity of the Holy Spirit, to seek to discover how God sees our situation, and what he would have us do. That is rather different from looking for an 'answer' which might be filed away and forgotten.

As we think about topical preaching, we can usefully consider the ministry of *the prophet*. It is a ministry in its own right, and not a sub-division of any style of preaching. Yet it closely relates to topical preaching. Indeed, the great prophets of the Old Testament functioned in exactly this way. Amos the countryman came to the city and was appalled by what he saw. He had no option but to speak out in the name of the Lord. In the Old Testament the prophet observes the situation of the people and senses their attitudes, and relates this to the holiness of their Lord.

There are usually two facets to prophecy, one relating to the present and the other to the future. The prophet is often able to speak of what the Lord will do. Thus for Amos there is first the condemnation of social sins, and then the foretelling of judgement (4:1-2). The famous 'Immanuel' passage in Isaiah 7 upbraids the king for his lack of faith and foretells that within a brief time Israel's enemies will be overthrown. Christians believe that Isaiah spoke more than he knew, and see a greater fulfilment in the coming of Jesus Christ, 'God with us' (Matthew 1:23).

There is prophecy in the New Testament, and Paul refers to its place in worship in 1 Corinthians 14:3. The emphasis appears to be on 'foretelling', for in Acts 21:10-11 the prophet Agabus speaks of what Paul will have to suffer in Jerusalem, and engages in a piece of prophetic symbolism by means of Paul's belt.

Prophecy occurs today, in both forms of present and future significance. Christian preachers have suffered persecution for speaking out against the injustice of apartheid in Africa. So there may be times when a preacher needs to point out injustice for what it is, perhaps at considerable personal cost. But prophecy can also be of encouragement to a local congregation when pointing to the future. A lay preacher found herself led to say of a church that God would keep sending new people to it; the church itself must be constantly ready and willing to receive. Over a lengthy period that has remained true. It could lead to complacency; it ought to be a cause of thankfulness and preparation.

Some of us may recoil from the thought of being prophets. We simply may not see ourselves in such a role, and in any case it might call for more moral courage than we possess. Others ought to beware of grasping the prophet's mantle too readily. If we are negative or scolding by nature, it may be too easy to fulminate against sin (not least if the perpetrators are not present) or to ride our own hobby-horse about what ought or ought not to be done in church. There may, however, be times when every one of us ought to accept the task of being a prophet. We need to come to the task humbly, with a certain reluctance, and with a determination to speak only when God gives the command. But if and when he does speak in this way, we must obey.

Yet how will we know that this conviction is from God, and not merely something of our own? One test may be the urgency of the impression within us. The prophet Jeremiah talked about 'a fire shut up in my bones' (20:9), which he could not hold in. If that is how you feel, count to ten, and inquire of yourself whether this might just possibly be an excuse for an ego-trip. Are you negative or scolding by nature? If you remain positive about the need to speak, share the conviction with three or four others, both people who understand you and those who may be likely to see things from a different point of view. See how you feel after doing that. If you then believe that you ought to go ahead, make sure of your facts (if there are any involved in the situation), pray quite specifically about the message you believe you have, and be open to respond in whatever way you may then be nudged by God. Overall, remember that what you do and say should all be done in a spirit of love.

(3) *Experiential Preaching*

Much of what has been said about topical preaching applies also to experiential preaching. Our experiences in life go to make up the persons we are and are still in the process of becoming. Reflection on these experiences can be an important part of understanding and growth, and in the Christian life it is important to stand back and seek to appreciate what God has been doing for us.

Christian experience is a vital part of faith, yet at the same time it can be a dangerous area. It is saddening to hear someone say that they have never been aware of God's presence in their life. Their believing really is a matter of faith and of faith alone. They have gone on doggedly with the journey. But on the other hand it is uncomfortable to listen to someone whose spirituality is largely a matter of 'feeling', and who is likely to jump on the latest religious bandwagon, if it seems to offer some titillation to the everyday demands of believing. The Christian life must be constantly reviewed in the light of the New Testament. There used to be a simple rule of thumb: Facts, Faith and Feelings. There are the facts about Christ as set out in the New Testament; we respond with faith, and 'feelings' emerge as the Lord directs and encourages our discipleship. The correct order for the three is vital. Get them out of order and there will be trouble. Experience is valid when it genuinely relates to the biblical revelation. Paul asserts that part of the work of the Holy Spirit is to testify 'with our spirit that we are God's children' (Romans 8:16).

There are dangers inherent in experiential preaching. My experience may be limited, self-centred or not typical of that of my congregation. I may be immature, both as a person and as a Christian. Is it right to share that? Further, by preaching on 'experience' do I unduly pander to an age which rejects absolutes and seeks only the immediate? Again, if a balanced gospel is to be offered, there may be times when I must preach 'more than I know'. Creation, the final judgement, heaven, and even the further stages of growing in grace are matters beyond my immediate awareness, and in order to deal with them I shall need to turn to the revelation offered by the Bible as well as my present insights and experience.

There are values in experiential preaching, however. Provided that you know something of the congregation, you can (as with topical preaching) start 'where people are'. You then go on to show the relevance of the Bible to what is happening to them.

There is also the fact that experiential preaching may enable you to deal in a direct way with the query whether Christianity has anything to offer in practical terms. If the age in which we live asks: 'What is there in this for me?', we need somehow to respond. Part of the effectiveness of evangelists such as Luis Palau and the Anglican J John is that they set out a practical issue (such as honesty at work or sexual relationships) and relate the Bible's teaching to it.

For the Christian, there can be value at times in analysing life into the 'spiritual' and the 'secular'. But the important thing is that the two should be one: part of the growth into spiritual maturity demands this. So there will be part of me that is dependent on prayer, Bible study, fellowship, worship, good relationships; whilst another part is concerned with earning my living and being keenly interested in football or the operatic society. The importance is that the former should affect the latter, and direct the way in which I perform my duties or enjoy my leisure. What emerges from this is that, for the preacher, any experience may be valid (and of value) in preaching, but every experience must be tested against what Jesus has revealed about the God who is love.

For example, a preacher finds that one of the set lessons for the day is Mark 10:2-16 (27th Sunday in Ordinary Time in Year B), where the subject of divorce is touched on. He or she has been through the pain of marriage deterioration and divorce. Does one avoid the issue? Or could it be dealt with as an 'academic' subject? Or does one acknowledge publicly (what the congregation doubtless already knows) that this is an area of deep personal experience? If it is possible to adopt such an approach, some of the difficulties could be shared, albeit with due brevity and sensitivity. Within this experience was there some way in which God's grace made 'all the difference', in terms of being able to understand the other person, being freed from bitterness, being able to forgive? A piece of expository preaching and an element of the experiential could be helpfully combined.

There is value too in sharing the common experience of the Christian community. Imagine a group of women in a rural area, spending a retreat day together. Most of them are married to sheep farmers. Their minister is asked to speak to them about Psalm 23. He does his preparation, but is aware that the group knows far more about sheep and shepherding than he does. So he asks them to share what they believe to be the characteristics of a good shepherd. Amongst about twenty qualities which they list are courage, dependability, concern for the sheep (beyond what might be dictated by economic factors), commitment to the task and selflessness. They have seen these things in the life of their families. They also speak about sheep: stubborn and stupid are the first words used. The conversation gradually moves from their experience on the farm to the description of God in the psalm, to Jesus' claim to be the good shepherd, and their awareness of being valued and cared for by him. The day culminates in worship, with the sermon preached by the minister. But what he says has been shaped by the shared experience.

The experiential sermon may also be developed from written accounts of Christian faith. What we read about others may lead us to preach about what they have discovered, with appropriate biblical comment. For example:

(i) St Augustine of Hippo in North Africa had rejected the Christian faith as a young man, experienced considerable inner turmoil, and then discovered God's presence. You may find his *Confessions* (an autobiography) or *City of God* hard work; but a source book such as the *Oxford Dictionary of Saints* or the *Oxford Dictionary of the Christian Church* will help you assimilate the essentials. Speak about him, fairly concisely, and then consider (in the light of the Bible) what he had discovered about human sin, the grace of God, and the overwhelming purposes of God even in the darkest moments of human history.

(ii) A more recent story which has captured the imagination of many is Jackie Pullinger's account of her work in Hong Kong in her books *Chasing the Dragon* and *Crack in the Wall*.[6] People released from the power of drugs, work done in the name of God against incredible odds, and the power of the Holy Spirit in ordinary lives, all feature here. What do we see in these accounts of the Bible's message being realised in our own time? What may be the implications for a typical congregation in a very different setting?

(iii) The story of Terry Waite has also been of inspiration to many.[7] As 'special envoy' of the Archbishop of Canterbury, he moved about the Middle East seeking to effect reconciliation. Captured in Beirut, and held for over four years (mostly in solitary confinement), his faith held and was fed by memorised Bible passages. There was also a postcard featuring a picture of John Bunyan in a prison cell. It came from a complete stranger, and was the one piece of mail to reach him in his captivity. God present in one's solitariness; faith sustained day after day when hope seemed impossible; love and forgiveness offered to one's captors: these are biblical themes worth developing from the experience which Terry Waite has shared with us.

Experiential preaching will probably be of most value where the subjects come from the congregation itself. A group of leaders will know the issues which are being faced, both personal and communal. They can suggest these from time to time to the minister or visiting preacher, whose task will be to relate them to the biblical material. Analysis and understanding of the experience can be set alongside relevant theology, and either affirmed, or shown to be defective, against the wider Christian backdrop.

The American preacher Harry Emerson Fosdick had a sermon with the intriguing title: 'Are you part of the world's problem or its answer?' The question invited immediate response, with a degree of self-examination. We all know about the world's problems, and mostly assume that they are caused by other people. We probably want to believe that we are part of the answer. But the Bible claims that we are all part of the problem. We all share the sinfulness which is at the root of the world's distress. To move towards Psalm 51 will show our need to acknowledge our sin and then discover the possibility of forgiveness. In Christ (as we see him in such passages as Mark 2:1-12) we find the renewal we need. The experience with which we began has been placed alongside what the Bible has to say.

Before we leave the subject of varieties of approach, we can add two more possibilities.

The first is to acknowledge that in the example of the women sharing their insights into shepherding we have what may be called a *group sermon*. It was the work of several people, though in the event only one person actually preached. It would not be a pattern for use every Sunday, but on special occasions, not least at conferences and retreats, it has real value. At one level, the group has acted like a Bible study fellowship, but the 'findings' have been collated and adapted for use in an act of worship. It takes a little skill to do the collating, and there may be times when the person who does this (probably the preacher) will need to mould what is said. That perhaps does not matter, since people are usually quite impressed to hear later what they have shared.

A second way in which we can diverge from the custom of having only one person responsible for the sermon is in the rarely used *dialogue sermon*. In the Middle Ages the Church set out to define doctrine by means of the disputation, in which one person argued a thesis and another challenged the position. One London city church used to run a highly successful lunchtime meeting for workers, in which the rector would question a visiting speaker. Sometimes the theme was general or political, but often was specifically Christian.

There are different ways of using the dialogue.

(i) There can be a straightforward question and answer, especially where someone known to the congregation has been through an experience (probably stressful) which has for them brought new insight and depth to living. Here we have the experiential approach in slightly different guise.

(ii) Someone with genuine knowledge or expertise can be interviewed, so as to impart information in an accessible way.

(iii) There can be something like a debate, with two people offering different viewpoints as a question is explored.

There are those who would want to keep fairly narrowly to a definition of preaching as the expression of 'truth through personality'. Probably the dialogue sermon, with the element of argument that it may contain, does not fall completely within that definition. But it can be of considerable value on the right occasion, not least when a church is faced with strongly held views on a controversial subject. Two factors must be borne in mind. One is that the dialogue sermon is a sermon and not a debate. If it concludes without offering a clear conclusion that very fact can lead to worthwhile prayer as the church seeks guidance. The second factor is that the dialogue needs a good deal of preparation. Especially where two people are offering different views, there is a need for discipline. Each must be willing to speak briefly so that the other may respond appropriately. Link phrases need to be planned and responded to, and respect and charity are essential.

We have been looking at a variety of approaches in our preaching. Wherever we begin, and however we develop the sermon, the aim is basically the same. One piece of advice given to preachers used to be: wherever you start, make haste across country to Jesus Christ. Whatever approach may be adopted in the cause of relevance or freshness, our aim is to open up the Bible message in such a way as to inform minds and strengthen hearts and wills in Christian discipleship.

4

VARIETY OF PURPOSE

A group of young people asked to be allowed to lead worship in their church. They produced a fairly predictable blend of hymns, prayers and readings, but decided that there would be no sermon. Instead – in a church where there was room to move and to display appropriately – they created three tableaux showing their vision for the world. First, they portrayed a world of peace. Second, they showed a world of sufficiency where all was properly shared. Finally, out of genuine conviction, they set out a world where all people brought their worship and allegiance to a caring God, revealed in Jesus. They were expressing their own hopes, and they thrilled the congregation. Their offering in worship showed purpose in creation, and had a clear message.

The purpose of every sermon ought in some way to be the encouraging and nurturing of Christian faith. God's grace remains unchanging, yet the way in which we present it on any given occasion may vary greatly.

William Sangster's *The Craft of Sermon Construction* was first published as long ago as 1949, but his classification of sermons with regard to their subject matter remains well worth considering. Sangster analysed sermons in six ways:

(1) Biblical Interpretation
(2) Ethical and Devotional
(3) Doctrinal
(4) Philosophic and Apologetic

(5) Social
(6) Evangelistic

Those aspects can firmly undergird any ministry of pastoral preaching. People need to be taught and nourished, and that will not be achieved by the repetition of a few themes dear to the preacher. Those who have the responsibility of facing the same congregation regularly need to work at providing a proper balance. But those who preach only occasionally to the same people are in a similar position. People have good memories, and will know if we deal with only one type of sermon. If we are predictable, effectiveness will be lost. Variety is important, not for its own sake but in the cause of achieving our purpose.

As we acknowledge the value of Sangster's analysis, we can adopt a somewhat simpler classification. We shall look at the three aspects of Teaching, Devotional, and Apologetic and Evangelistic. To these we can add a category of special services which make their own demand.

(1) *Teaching*

Even long-established church members are willing to admit (as we have already noted) that they are ignorant of many parts of the Christian faith. They are unsure about what they are 'supposed to believe', and do not know how best to remedy this. Reading is one answer, but although there are plenty of Christian books available, few contain comprehensive teaching in an accessible and reliable form. In any case, the habit of reading is not one that everyone possesses. The twenty minutes slot on Sunday is an ideal time for clear and consistent teaching. It will make demands on the preacher, but they should be gladly accepted.

All this presupposes that there *is* a body of truth that the Church possesses, and which is relevant to the needs of contemporary people. There is good argument for the claim that what God is like, as we see him in the life and teaching of Jesus Christ, is the basic truth which remains valid amidst the overwhelming advances of modern knowledge. The biblical insights into creation, the responsibility of humankind for the world in which it lives, caring within the community, forgiveness, acceptance by God, growth in personality, providential care, all speak to our present condition. The biblical vision of an existence where all evil is destroyed, and praise and joy are centred on God, is one which can provide a driving force within a world of greed, suffering and neglect. It is a matter of using the imagination to preach on such themes as they touch on contemporary events. A single sermon, or series of sermons, can provide material for the believer to see such affairs through the spectacles of the gospel.

Once again we are moving into the realm of co-operation between preachers. Where we take a large subject that demands several sermons, lay and ministerial colleagues can share over a number of Sundays. The effect of such team work is often greatly valued by a congregation.

Subjects for teaching sermons are virtually endless. The following are some typical possibilities.

(a) The phrases from the old prayer of *General Thanksgiving* offer an outline for a four-part series. What does the Bible teach about (i) our creation; (ii) our preservation through the varied experiences of life; (iii) all the blessings of life granted to us (and our stewardship of them); and (iv) the redemption as we experience it in Christ, not just in personal terms but in God's grand plan for the whole of his creation? The prayer also refers to the means of grace, a theme in itself.

(b) Given the increased awareness in recent years of the work of *the Holy Spirit* many congregations would appreciate some consistent teaching about his activity.

 (i) What did Jesus teach his disciples to expect that the Spirit would do for them?

 (ii) What difference did his coming at Pentecost make to the disciples?

(iii) What are the graces of Christian character imparted by the Spirit? (ie. Galatians 5:22-23).
(iv) What gifts for Christian service does the Spirit bring? (ie. 1 Corinthians 12 and elsewhere). People are usually responsive when the graces of character are set out before them, and when it is explained how God wants to equip them for service.

(c) There are many ways of dealing with *the life and teaching of Jesus*. Series can be developed about his life of prayer, his declaration of the kingdom of God, the claims he made in the 'I am' sayings of John's gospel, the theological implications of what Paul sets out in Philippians 2:6-11, Jesus as preacher/teacher/healer/Lord in the gospels.

(d) At *Communion services* (even if the sermon is only of three minutes duration) there could be a series on the meaning of the sacrament, as memorial, thanksgiving, fellowship meal, symbol of the Lord's presence with his people. Just as now it is customary for lay persons to share in the administration of this sacrament, so it can be fitting for a lay preacher to share in the Communion preaching.

(e) *Revelation 1-3* has often been used for a teaching series, with its vision of the Lord of the Church and then the seven letters to the churches in Asia. In his translation of these letters, J B Phillips offers helpful descriptions of each of the churches: [2]

(i)	Ephesus	– the loveless church
(ii)	Smyrna	– the persecuted church
(iii)	Pergamum	– the over-tolerant church
(iv)	Thyatira	– the compromising church
(v)	Sardis	– the sleeping church
(vi)	Philadelphia	– the church with opportunity
(vii)	Laodicea	– the complacent church.

These adjectives should enable us to relate the letters to our condition today.

(f) The little book of *Ruth* has been called 'an everyday story of country folk', echoing the sub-title given to *The Archers* serial on BBC radio. Its four chapters contain a theme of loyalty, through which God is able to work in the highly unsatisfactory times of the Judges. There is Ruth's loyalty to her mother-in-law and the customs of the new people amongst whom she has come to live, Boaz's loyalty to the demands of the laws of kinship, and God's loyalty to faithful people who set out to serve him in ordinary affairs. There is material here about guidance and providence, and the way in which God works in situations that may seem at the time to have little significance.

The teaching sermon will demand of the preacher a considerable understanding of the Bible background, and will probably involve a good deal of reading. There will be times when questions must be raised and have to be left without definite answers. But the purpose will be to attempt to state positively what Christian belief is. There should be no escaping the hard questions, nor must there be oversimplification. Clear points are called for, and a practical application. Good teaching informs and stimulates further thought.

(2) *Devotional*

The word 'devotional' is sometimes devalued by the assumption that it has to do with a certain kind of religious sentimentality or sloppiness. There may be some justification for that attitude. Some of us may well have been guilty on occasion of thinking that we have 'only a devotional address' to give, and the preparation was therefore less stringent than it ought to have been.

Dictionaries relate devotion to words such as dedication, consecration and applying oneself completely to a task or person. William Sangster linked devotional sermons with the ethical. For him they were concerned with the building up of Christian character. He also associated them with comfort and encouragement. They are to take us further down the Christian road, and he claimed that 'they are calculated most especially for the help of those who are "all out" for the holy life'.³

What we are aiming at in the devotional sermon is *encouragement*, and that has less to do with sentimentality than with challenge. Barnabas is presented in the New Testament as one who encouraged others to greater maturity in faith, and the devotional sermon will seek to do the same. There ought to be nothing tepid about it, nor at the same time anything discouraging. One congregation said to a new minister: 'Please don't scold us. For years people have been telling us what to do. We have tried to listen, but the agenda has grown longer and longer and we really haven't the energy to respond.' No doubt it was good that they had been challenged, but realism should have been linked with the demands. It was essential not only to point the congregation to what they ought to be doing, but also to show them the resources of faith and strength in which they could face up to the demands of Christian discipleship.

As we attempt this ministry of encouragement it is worth remembering the meaning of the Greek word *Parakletos* which John's gospel uses of the Holy Spirit. It relates to consolation and comfort, hence the use of 'Comforter' as a description of the Spirit in some translations. But it has to do with exhortation and encouragement, perhaps a rather stronger concept. The Spirit acts as a pace-maker may do in a race. The object is not to discourage the other runners, but to draw out their very best; and part of the ministry of encouragement by the preacher is to show that the Lord who makes demands is also the one who enables.

The letter of Paul to the Philippians is a good source for devotional preaching, and in fact a splendid example of a pastor encouraging his people. The church at Philippi knew squabbles and divisions. Things were going wrong for them, yet they had the virtue of a genuine concern for Paul, who was in prison and in possible danger of his life. Paul's response was to be expressly grateful for what they had done for him. He pointed them away from their divisions to the kind of self-giving exemplified in the life and ministry of

Jesus. He encouraged them to believe that the Lord was always at hand and could be known directly in prayer. The believer could cope with anything because of the presence of the one who strengthened him. Paul suggests that his only ambition is to enjoy the fellowship of Christ (with all that that will demand in suffering for others), and that he has come to learn the secret of contentment. What Paul has discovered may be the possession of the Philippians also.

The devotional sermon is appropriate at a celebration of Holy Communion, and at services where there is prayer and laying on of hands for healing. In such worship it ought to be clear that what we do is not a matter of our own worthiness. God is offering his gracious love, freely. Even the briefest of sermons on such occasions can point confidently to this grace. The account of Jesus being called to the emergency of Jairus' daughter's illness tells of a woman in the crowd, whom Jesus singled out to assure of healing and peace (Mark 5:25-34). That same assurance is for God's people now. St Augustine said to God: 'Command what you will. Give what you command.' Good devotional preaching depends on good theology. It will ensure that the relationship with Christ is seen not as a burden but as a privilege in which strength is received.

(3) *Apologetic and Evangelistic*

Every follower of Christ is called to be a witness. A man who had been healed was told to go home, to the people who knew him best, and tell them the great things that the Lord had done for him (Mark 5:19). Similarly a blind man who was healed spoke of what had happened, even though he did not understand it: 'One thing I do know. I was blind but now I see' (John 9:25). Even the least articulate has the responsibility of speaking about the faith.

The readers of 1 Peter are challenged to go a step further, however. They must be 'prepared to give an answer to everyone who asks you to give the reasons for the hope you have' (3:15). The Greek word translated 'answer' is *apologia*, a speech for the defence. Although this gives us the word 'apology' in English, it is stronger and more pro-active in Christian use. We are not 'excusing' the fact that we believe, but setting out clearly our reasons for doing so.

Thus the Christian is to be a witness and an apologist. The same is true of the preacher. In what we say there ought to be an element of underlying conviction that makes it apparent that we *know* what we are talking about. There ought also to be an indication that we have carefully worked through the reasons for the claims that we are making.

We can acknowledge that there are some preachers who have particular gifts in these two areas, though rarely does one person excel in both. The New Testament lists the ministry of evangelists as a gift of the Holy Spirit (Ephesians 4:11), and there are some preachers (not necessarily the most eloquent) who have this ability of enabling people to come to a living faith. When they preach, people respond: the claims of Christ have been so presented that a response of heart, mind and will is achieved. Some of these preachers are household names, whilst others are little-known outside their own locality.

Similarly there are those who seem able to set out a rationale for the Christian faith with particular effectiveness. For some seventy years Donald Soper 'reasoned' patiently with all and sundry in the open air. An ability to deal with superficial hecklers was a great help; but the work could only be done in the light of constant reflection on both Christianity and contemporary affairs.

A classic example of apologetics and evangelism going hand-in-hand is found in the ministry of Philip the evangelist in the Acts of the Apostles (8:26-39). Philip answers the question raised by the Ethiopian: he relates the Old Testament passage which is being read to the life and work of Jesus. Relevant apologetics answers the question that is being asked. Then Philip responds to the African in his request for baptism. He has expounded the good news of what Jesus may mean for him, and helped him to an act of faith. That is the work of the evangelist.

But if we acknowledge that there are those who are gifted in the areas of apologetics and of evangelism, that does not excuse the rest of us from the tasks. We may not match the skills of the 'experts', but we are nevertheless called to exercise our ministry in both spheres. There used to be a custom of placing in pulpits a card on which were inscribed the words 'Sir, we would see Jesus' from John 12:21. It is a legitimate, indeed vital, request to the preacher. Whatever may be the thrust or content of our sermon, our aim is to point to Christ.

A key issue in the matter of apologetics is that of what questions we should be trying to answer. It is often said of preachers that we want to answer the questions that no one is asking. Certainly we all have the temptation of shying away from the hard questions, and dealing only with those we think we can cope with. When we set out on the task of the apologist we need to make sure that what we speak about is relevant to the congregation's needs. It is they who must set the agenda. A tragedy has occurred in the life of a church family or in the neighbourhood. Can we face the challenge of preaching about this, or at any rate setting aside a part of the sermon to give sensitive comment? There may be something in the book of Job which has spoken to us and which is worth sharing. Or there is Psalm 73 with its questionings about the unfairness of life but its movement towards faith as the writer sees human affairs in the perspective of God's activity. Or perhaps Habakkuk can help. He is honest enough to complain that God seems to pay no heed to the bad things that are happening. Yet still he manages to conclude with the sublime statement of faith in 3:17-18. There is Jesus' experience of darkness and rejection on the cross in Mark 15:34. Does this open up any understanding which helps in the worst of days? Paul found help from God in the worst of times, and was able to share it (2 Corinthians 1:3-11). Perhaps the less fitted we feel to respond to a tragic pastoral situation, the more we may be used to be a channel of help to others.

Part of the task of the apologist is to find images which have some resonance in the mind of the average person (whoever that may be!) The Bible images of God as parent (though this is not helpful to all), gardener and potter may help, just as the image of a good steward can relate to the growing concern for responsible living on this planet. Each of us can try to be imaginative about new images which could be of value. Most of us will need to rely on the help of people who know more about a specific subject than we do. But if you are going to speak on an issue where scientific facts are vital for a proper understanding, there is probably someone to whom you may turn for an 'idiot's guide', and who will be more than glad to give you the time you need.

Our aim in apologetics and evangelism is to bring people to a true faith in Christ. Those who are gifted as evangelists sometimes make use of the 'altar call', where individuals are invited to come to the front of the church as an overt sign of their response. For some this open acknowledgement of faith is of value. It will certainly open up the opportunity for personal counselling. Even if we do not see this ministry of public invitation as ours, we ought to feel a responsibility of enabling those who hear us to make a commitment to the Lord. There is frequent complaint that preachers do not build enough silence into worship. It may therefore be that silence is a fitting way to conclude a sermon where we have been calling for faith. Perhaps a few (very few) quiet and sympathetic suggestions for prayer may be apposite; but then should follow a time to allow people to make a specific response to God.

(4) *The Special Occasion*

Besides the three aspects that we have considered, and the purposes which lie behind those different types of sermons, we need also to look at the special occasion. The theme and style of the sermon are thrust on the preacher because of some occurrence, personal, local or national. What needs to be said will almost certainly be covered by the three categories we have thought about; but particular occasions will make their own demands and necessitate a blend perhaps of all three areas of teaching, devotional, and apologetic and evangelistic.

(a) We commonly join baptisms, weddings and funerals under the heading of *rites of passage*. They lie deep in the development of our lives. Each makes its different demand on the preacher; but to link the three has the merit of drawing attention to the fact that they are often performed, as it were, on the circumference of church life. Most of those present are likely to have little regular link with a church; indeed, some may never have been inside a church before. This is to make no judgement, but is rather to remind us as preachers of the dual concern to remain faithful to our message, and at the same time to be aware of the background of those to whom we shall be speaking. A lay preacher may rarely have the opportunity of speaking at these services, though where there are family or other links his or her personal contribution may be crucial.

Whilst it is hoped that a service of *baptism* will take place within the regular worship of the church, that is not always possible. It may be necessary to hold a special service, perhaps for one child, perhaps for several. If an infant is being brought for baptism, what is said will depend on whether the parents are regular members of the church community. If they are, then there will be a background against which Jesus' acceptance of the small children for blessing (Mark 10:13-16) or the commission in Matthew 28:19 can be expounded. Within regular worship a sermon on baptism can be a timely reminder of the themes of God's grace, decision in Christian discipleship, the need for cleansing of our sin, and the concern that the Church ought to have for children (and for the more mature newly-baptised). Where the baptism is performed in a 'private' ceremony, outside regular worship, there is a strong argument that a brief (three minutes) sermon ought to be included, in order that the sacrament should not be seen as a piece of sentimentality attached to the proper delight in the arrival of a new child. The theme will best be something direct, and relate to our need of cleansing or of the parents' thanksgiving and responsibilities. We are in debt to a loving God. What we say can be a blend of evangelism and apologetic, perhaps with reference to a topical news item. It will need careful preparation if we are to keep within the time.

Where the baptism is that of an adult, there is a quite different situation. One of the moments of baptism recorded in the New Testament could be used, or the symbolism of our dying and rising to new life in Christ, which Paul sets out in Romans 6:3-4.

The opportunity of speaking at a *marriage* ceremony is one of the great privileges of the preacher. Such an important occasion in the lives of two people and of their families deserves our best. In an age when marriage is at a discount, the fact that this couple have opted for it is significant. But we have to be sensitive about the background. Is this a first or subsequent marriage? What is the attitude of the families? What degree – if any – of Christian understanding and commitment do bride and groom possess? As always, the challenge is to find some link between the situation and the good news of the Bible. The fact that love is one of God's gifts to us; the need to work at relationships if they are to be strong and lasting; the grace of being able to forgive – and to be forgiven; the joy of discovering oneself in self-giving, are relevant themes. The story of Jesus' presence at the wedding in Cana (John 2) may help, or Paul's picture of the clothes which fit the relationship which God desires of us (Colossians 3:12); or it may be some aspect of the moving description of Christian love in 1 Corinthians 13, where the ingredients of a lasting relationship are set out. It scarcely needs saying that the emphasis ought to be on the celebration of joy and hopefulness.

It is trite to say that the one certain thing about life is death. But the Christian knows that whilst on the one hand there is tragedy in the statement (not least in that the Bible links our mortality with our sinfulness), on the other this event speaks to us of the opening up of richer life in Christ. To speak at a *funeral* is therefore an awesome task, and as one comments (however briefly and inadequately) on the life of a fellow human being, it is also important to set that life within the gracious providence of God. Pastorally it is vital to make links with the family, where they have not been known previously. It is important to be aware of the interests of the deceased. It is not unknown for a minister to assume that only a handful of mourners will be present, and then to find that there is a large congregation representing professional, sports or service interests who have come to pay their tribute. There may also be associations only recently discovered by the family, where a person has been away for a long time. We need to be able to respond sensitively, and to find a fitting word to say about the Christian hope.

It can be an embarrassment if the funeral address becomes an uncritical eulogy which suggests that the greatest of Christian saints has just left this earthly life. We can be grateful that no longer is it customary to speculate on the destination of the deceased. A sympathetic appreciation of the main aspects of his or her life, with perhaps a touch of humour to cover those areas which fell somewhat short of perfection, ought to suffice. Where possible it is good to relate the life to some relevant area of biblical spirituality. For example:

(i) it is said of Levi that he was a man of integrity and peace (Malachi 2:6)

(ii) Mary is commended as being one who quietly listened to what Jesus had to say (Luke 10:42)

(iii) Dorcas was remembered as a person who was concerned in practical terms for those less well-off than herself (Acts 9:36)

(iv) Barnabas is shown as a mature Christian, 'a good man, full of the Holy Spirit and faith' (Acts 11:24)

(v) Epaphroditus had proved his Christian loyalty as a 'brother, fellow-worker and fellow-soldier' (Philippians 2:25)

Especially where there is deep grief, it may be of help to refer to Jesus' own ministry (as in the story of Jairus' daughter in Mark 5:21-43, and in the case of the widow's son at Nain in Luke 7:11-15), and not least to his own sense of loss in the death of his friend Lazarus, which brought him to tears (John 11:35). Where there is tragedy and a feeling that a life has been cut short in its prime, there may be need for reassurance. Psalm 23 may help, as may Psalm 33:11 with its awareness of God's purposes not being frustrated.

Some of us are long-winded, and a funeral service must be a reminder of the discipline of time. At a crematorium, the service time is strictly limited, and will probably not allow for even ten minutes of tribute-cum-sermon. But three minutes, well used, will enable people to acknowledge and give thanks for a loved one or friend whom they release into God's care, and to leave the chapel feeling that they have been to a Christian service.

Even if most lay preachers will never be called on to speak at a funeral service, there will be times when during normal Sunday worship they will be confronted by those who are mourning, sometimes in a large family group. When the preacher has been duly informed beforehand, at least a small part of the sermon material can be adapted to cover the needs of those who grieve, and to underline the hope that we have as Christians. Where notice has not been given, and we are caught unprepared, it is possible to refer to the family's presence at some point in the service, and to use time in the prayers in an appropriate way.

(b) There is a whole range of special occasions of *local*, *national* or even *international* importance where the preacher will be expected to speak. Remembrance Sunday services may be celebrated in church, or in the open air at some civic venue. The theme is fairly specific, and there are many passages in the Bible which fit in, for God's people have been given a vision not only of the world as it is but as God plans it to be. Psalm 85:10 talks of how 'love and faithfulness meet together; righteousness and peace kiss each other'. The psalmist is realistic enough to know that humankind has forfeited those gifts from the Lord, but looks in faith to God for better things.

But national and civic occasions are not always neatly written into our diaries, giving the opportunity to prepare satisfactorily. Crises and tragedies arrive unexpectedly, demanding an immediate response, however ill-prepared we may feel. The accidental death of Diana, Princess of

Wales in 1997 occurred late on a Saturday night. Some people arriving at church a few hours later were not even aware of the fact. How ought preachers to have responded in the services that morning? For most there was little that could be done other than a brief comment in the sermon, and the use of the prayers in an appropriate way. Had there been two or three days before the Sunday in which to prepare a different theme, it would have enabled the preacher to try to deal with such matters as grief, the fragility of human existence, what contribution we may make through our concerns for others, providence, and Christian belief in life beyond death. The purpose would be, as in the whole act of worship, to enable the congregation to face a sense of shock and loss in the presence of God, to offer this to him, and to seek to draw insight and encouragement from the gospel message.

There may be moments when the less the preacher has to say, the better it will be. On Tyneside the much-loved lay preacher Winship Storey found himself conducting worship at a large suburban church on the morning of 3rd September, 1939. As the service began, war was declared against Germany. Memories of the horrors of previous conflicts, especially the first world war of 1914-18, filled the minds of the more elderly worshippers. Winship Storey scrapped his prepared theme, and instead of preaching invited the people to listen to some of the great biblical passages which speak of the dependability of God and of his supreme purposes of love and salvation as they straddle even the worst events of human history.

However, the appropriate theme may not always be one of comfort. We must be prepared to be unpopular, if need be. In Old Testament times there were prophets who wanted to cry 'Peace!' to the people when God had other words to say. Though most of us will recoil from the role of prophet if it means saying hard things, there are times when it is unavoidable. As the Falklands War closed in 1982, there was rightly an expectation that the nation should give thanks. But those responsible for the official service in London's St Paul's Cathedral found themselves unable to share the unalloyed joy of some politicians and military people. So in the service the British victory was not stressed. There was no triumphalism, and concern was shown for the Argentinian people in their defeat. What might have been a natural political response was being tempered by biblical themes of forgiveness and compassion. Some national leaders were highly critical. So the preacher who always says what people want to hear is on dangerous ground. There may be times when we need to assert that the spirit of the age, even of our hearers, is out of tune with the spirit of Christ.

(c) Most of the special services at which we are asked to preach will be within *the local church's calendar,* or at any rate within the realm of related organisations such as Christian Aid. Each church has its own list. Apart from the liturgical round of the Christian year there are services for missions, women, men, young people, the choir, guilds and other parts of the church family. There will probably be a Church Anniversary and almost certainly Harvest thanksgiving. Occasionally a dispirited preacher has been known to murmur that there ought to be a special Sunday simply for preaching the gospel. The task for anyone asked to preach at a 'special' service is basically two-fold: (i) to take the event seriously, by trying to understand the purposes and work of the group, which will involve gathering as much background information as possible; and (ii) to discover how the good news of Christ applies to this, in order to help the members find their place in the mission of the church and the life of the community around. We are to help people see beyond the commitment to their group (which can be genuinely important in its own right, but may have the danger of inducing tunnel vision) to catch a wider vision of the purposes of God.

For example, on Choir Sunday you might speak about what Paul says in Colossians 3:16-17, where he talks of singing 'psalms, hymns and spiritual songs in your hearts to God' and goes on to claim that everything should be done in Christ's name in gratitude to God. Music is a most important part of our worship, and for many it helps towards an awareness of God's presence. Allied to the right words, it can enable us to express our gratitude and praise.

In the light of this, what is the purpose of a choir? It is not that of wanting to be the best group in the area, although it ought to be committed to being as good as it can. It is not simply a vehicle to enable musicians to find personal fulfilment, although it is to be hoped that they find pleasure in what they do. It is to enable God's people the better to express the praise of God, and the better it does this the more it will be playing its part in the total life and mission of the church in its neighbourhood.

★ ★ ★ ★ ★

A young man wanders into a church on a Sunday morning. He is not sure why he is there, for he has not been to church since he was a small boy. He is welcomed sincerely, and finds that the preacher seems to be speaking directly to him from a Bible passage. He is aware of the presence of God and the challenge to his life, and he becomes a Christian. That true story happens in some form or another week by week, and it is good to remind ourselves of what happens when God is at work. There may be a number of purposes which from time to time we seek to achieve in the pulpit. We shall teach and encourage and explain. But the basic purpose is that of awakening faith in Christ, followed by the building up of a new lifestyle. We believe ourselves to be called as preachers. Since God really is at work, we may expect results to follow, even from the poor offerings that we set before his people.

5

VARIETY OF PEOPLE AND PLACES

It was my first visit to the packed village chapel way up in the hills on the edge of the Lake District. There were many young people present, and it seemed that a reference to football might prove that the preacher was human. But which team did they support? Carlisle United was a fair way off, as were Blackpool and Preston North End. Surely we could not go wrong with Manchester United? Most people know the names of at least half-a-dozen of their star players. My attempts fell flat. There was little flicker of response in the congregation's eyes. Afterwards a kindly steward said: 'You'd have done better to talk about fell-running or sheep-dog trials.'

Each congregation is different, and we need – as far as may be possible – to do our homework about the people, their interests and their community. There used to be a saying: 'Take your best sermon to the country, and your best suit to the town.' Today the advice would be regarded as sexist, and perhaps even in its time it was unfair to the supposedly well-heeled suburban church. But it did serve as a warning never to dismiss anyone, or a small congregation, as not worthy of your best efforts.

(1) We need always to be conscious of the variety of people to whom we shall preach. One point of paramount importance is to preach at their level. Too many preachers are accused of preaching over people's heads. One steward

said of a preacher: 'His preaching is way above us. We like him, but we rarely understand what he is saying. In any case, what he is trying to say in no way seems to relate to our situation.' Contrast that with the people who said of someone that she always seemed to say just what they needed to hear, and in words that they could understand.

Why did the former preacher fail to communicate? Was it because he did not understand the wavelength on which the people operated? Was it because he was trying to stretch them, but failing in his teaching technique? Was it because he did not clearly think through, or clearly understand, what he wanted to say? There are different levels at which we may need to work. Some people want to hear an 'intellectual' sermon. But what may be a stimulating message in a university town may appear to have little relevance to a struggling church on a typical housing estate, and vice versa. Similarly, what may be an extremely helpful devotional sermon for a predominantly elderly group may be dismissed by a church of younger people who look for a message with some zest in it.

Having said that, it is well to remember that good teachers are able to communicate in such a way as not only to inform but also to leave people asking questions and making discoveries. People do understand what is being said, but at the same time are stretched. This teaching ability may be a gift, but even if it is not ours, we have the responsibility of endeavouring constantly to increase our skills of communication.

(2) In reality there are few churches which are monochrome and consist of one type of person, unless, unfortunately, the whole congregation is over sixty years of age. Interests, experiences and needs will be varied, and an important part of our preparation – where we have not been to the church before – ought to be to find out as much as we can about them. The monthly magazine or newsletter (where there is one) will help, as will booklets written for special occasions such as a centenary. A visit or telephone call to the organist or choir leader will reveal which hymns and music they prefer, with the spirituality that lies behind

them. What kind of community is the church set in, and do the church members actually reflect that community? The information you glean will help determine your themes and shape your approach. So, *discover the pattern.*

(3) Another matter for the preacher to be aware of is what stage people are at in their Christian lives. In practice, any congregation will contain a range of development, and a whole spectrum will need to be ministered to. One encouraging fact of current church life is that in many congregations there are *new Christians,* whose presence in the church can be measured in months or even weeks, rather than years. For them each Sunday can be a discovery of something new about the Christian faith. Their knowledge may be somewhat limited, and they may be understandably impatient of some of the attitudes and traditions of those who have been in the church for decades. But their enthusiasm, perhaps hard to channel at times, can be a tonic for other Christians. They have much to learn, and their very impatience may guide towards a reassessment of priorities. The preacher needs to fan the flame of new faith and not dismiss it as immaturity.

(4) Then there are those who are more *mature* in Christian experience. For some, there may be a sense of drifting, for they have reached a stage where the freshness departed long ago. They need encouragement to keep on with their journey, and part of this may come (ironically) from the more traditional elements in church life, not least as they are helped to look back at the experience both of the saints and of ordinary Christians of the past. They may be bewildered by, or even envious of, the people who have come new to faith. Our task is to offer them something which they know already, but which will come with a freshness that will enable them to say: 'Is that so? I had never seen it in that way before.'

One key which may enable this to happen may be in the outline of the sermon, which will stimulate fresh thought, or in the use of some modern illustration. For example, a staple part of the Christmas worship will be the account of the visit of the magi to Bethlehem, from Matthew 2. This is perhaps too well-known, especially where the gifts of gold, frankincense and myrrh lead to a sermon on Jesus' offices as king, priest and saviour. The interpretation is splendid, but predictable. But concede for a moment that these men (we are not told how many they were) were in fact kings, as popular tradition has it. The story can then be told in terms of what they represent (the quest of knowledge), what King Herod represents (the exercise of tyrannical power), and of what Jesus represents (God's kingdom of love). You may fairly preach about these three kingdoms. Knowledge is important, but has its limitations and can breed arrogance; power is important, but can become dangerous; whilst love is the essence of human existence and God's purpose. Charles Wesley brings the three together when he describes God as 'wisdom, power and love.'[1] The kingdoms find their true being in him who offers himself humbly in the incarnation. Such a sideways look may enable even a veteran sermon taster to realise something new.

The Methodist hymn book produced by John Wesley in 1780 contained a section related to Christian experience, and listed seven headings. They were about believers rejoicing, fighting, praying, watching, working, suffering and seeking. One group, shown this list, was somewhat amused by what they took to be its quaintness. But they then went on to acknowledge how aptly those verbs described their own situations from time to time. Their request was that they should be taken as sermon themes. They saw in them something helpful in their desire to become more mature Christians.

Some of the more mature Christians will be reaching the age when increasingly they think of the meaning of existence and in particular the possibility and quality of life after death. There is nothing morbid in this: it is a natural stage in our development. However, people often comment that they rarely, if ever, hear sermons on heaven. It may be that as preachers we deserve some credit for keeping our feet firmly on the ground, but the Bible does talk about our destiny in the presence of God, and we ought to say something about it, even if only around the time of All Saints day each year.

It is significant that recently many people over the age of sixty have found their way into church after many years away from it. It is as if they have looked at all the options and wonder whether after all there may be something in the Christian message. Too often our worship can be earthbound and our preaching related to what we take to be practical issues. The preacher needs sensitivity about those who want to reflect quietly on what they are beginning to see as the things that really matter. The Lord has made us not only for time, but also for eternity. Perhaps it is this questing for a more quiet style of reflective worship that makes some say that while they enjoy the vibrancy of morning worship with all ages present, they find also great value in a less well-attended evening service where quiet is possible. Some of us need that type of opportunity to reflect. One well-known broadcaster claims not to be conventionally religious, but says that when he feels in need of spiritual renewal he mentally transports himself to the Quaker Meeting House at Come-to-Good, near Truro in Cornwall, a place of great beauty and tranquillity. As preachers we shall do well to remember such needs.

(5) Sooner or later every preacher will be asked to lead *worship which is all-age*. The whole family of the church meets together and stays together in its praise and learning. Some of us have the gift of being at ease with children, and will not take this as an undue responsibility. For others the demands of preparation and the actual leadership will be onerous. One thing that can and ought to be done is co-operation with the local people, both in the preparation of the theme and act of worship, and in the service itself. Perhaps the lectionary or junior church material suggests a theme; but if not, there may be significant matters locally which offer a topical subject. The preacher may of course have his or her own ideas about a theme. Perhaps a well-known hymn can provide a framework for the service. For example, Doreen Newport's 'Think of a world without any flowers'[2] is set out in three parts. The first two verses relate to the natural world, the next four are concerned with people and with skills that they bring to our human experience, and the last two verses speak of the way in which God has come to us in Jesus Christ. These themes can be explained and

illustrated as the hymn is sung, section by section, throughout the service.

There will no doubt be people with gifts who can be used in the service, as worship leaders, helpers with visual aids or sharers in activity or dramatic presentation which takes the theme forward. Some may help with readings and perhaps even with speaking to the younger children if the preacher does not feel able to do this. This is not an abrogation of responsibility. The overall conduct of worship is still in your hands, but you are rightly using the gifts available in the church.

Where children are present throughout the service it is important to ask yourself how long the worship is to last. Anything over an hour is probably too long for all-age worship (unless you have remarkable gifts); fifty minutes may be about right, and in fact something quite worthy can be offered to God in only forty minutes.

The teaching needs to be relevant and crisp, with a maximum of fifteen minutes at a time. Perhaps the material will lend itself to being presented in three short talks of five minutes; or it could be divided into five minutes quite definitely aimed at younger children, and which they can respond to (perhaps through question and answer, or visual aids), followed later in the service by ten minutes on the same theme more specifically for the older people. Even that ten minutes needs to be highlighted by a good story or two, or to be material which is within the grasp of all ages, even if its deeper significance will be appreciated only by the adults.

(6) A significant and exciting development in British church life has been the emergence of the *multi-national church*. With immigration from throughout the Commonwealth, together with the loosening of boundaries more latterly within Europe, many congregations are now a fascinating mixture of nationality, colour and culture. Even a comparatively modest size of church may on a Sunday morning produce a gathering of over twenty nations and mother tongues. Because of our national reticence and

prejudices, we have not dealt with this opportunity very well, but in many places, not least in the inner city, the church has been given new life. Fresh traditions have been a stimulus, and often depth of belief and great love for the Lord have been gifts brought to a tired and despairing church.

As I go to preach in such a church, there are at least two things that must be in the forefront of my mind. (i) I am being reminded that I live on a large planet, not just in the 'little Britain' that is dear to me. At least in the prayers, if not in the sermon, I must remember what is happening far away. The motorway crash may be near at hand, but some worshippers will be torn by worry about families facing natural disasters or civil unrest in other continents. (ii) My language needs to be scrutinised, not just in terms of obviously racist remarks (albeit made thoughtlessly) but also concerning little 'in' jokes that only middle-aged or elderly English people might be expected to understand. My task is not to hurt my fellow-Christians, but to help them in their understanding of the gospel and also to receive from them as they share with me a wider perception of God's kingdom on earth.

Further, as people with experience of different cultures and other parts of the world become preachers, I shall discover that they have fresh insights into the Bible story which can enrich my own faith. My privilege is to share in a team which God has called from diverse backgrounds to speak a message of reconciliation, renewal and peace.

(7) Another matter is the question of *numbers*. In a sense they ought not to concern us, for Christ has spoken about being present with the 'two or three' (Matthew 18:20). There may be as much – or more – joy for the Lord in worship sincerely offered by a small group as that of a large congregation. Each person is important to God, and should be to us; and thus numbers are irrelevant.

It may be, though, that we can help a small group to realise that it is part of a worldwide church, and indeed a community belonging to the Lord which transcends time.

Size is in any case relative. One small chapel was discouraged that its Sunday attendance was 'only' sixteen; but when set in the context of a local community of fifty, it was an exceedingly large percentage. The small congregation has its own validity, with its pastoral and priestly ministry to its locality just as much as has a large cathedral. The preacher therefore needs to prepare just as diligently for the small as for the large church.

But there is a difference, and we shall do the small church (be it in country or in town) a disservice if we look on its worship as a scaled-down version of what is able to be done in a larger gathering with choir and organ. A simpler and more direct style of worship may be needed, but is just as important in its own right. The preacher may lack the rush of adrenalin (and touch of selfish excitement?) found in facing two or three hundred; but with a dozen or so, there can be eye-contact (unless we are tied to reading our notes), and this can be deeply rewarding. There can thus be more personal communication, and perhaps our personal integrity will be more open to our hearers. To preach to a small number is no easy option.

(8) It may be that as preachers we sometimes pitch our *expectations* too low. This is understandable if we know the place to which we are going, and have seen few signs of vitality over the years. But the gospel command to be expectant and alert ought not to be ignored.

Some of the toughest work for the church lies on housing estates on the edges of large cities. Numbers are small, leadership is scarce and often has to be drawn from outside the estate, which is far from ideal. But there is a conviction that the work is worthwhile. One such church was surprised one Sunday morning by the attendance of a middle-aged woman who lived locally. Her story, which she shared later, was straightforward. She had not been in church since she was a girl. Her whole life had been lived on the estate. Family life was now in tatters, with members in prison. Once again the weekend had come round, and she found herself saying: 'There must be more to life than this.' Instead of going to the shops to buy the newspapers, she dropped into the church. The lay preacher was talking about the way in which Christ calls people and offers a new quality of life. It made sense; she quietly responded; and she threw in her lot with these people. A new Christian was born, and her coming stimulated the congregation to look again at their work and expectations. As we go to preach, we need to maintain an awareness that Christ is alive and likely to act in unexpected ways.

(9) The housing estate is one of several *categories of churches*, each of which has varying needs. An emphasis on encouragement is appropriate for the estate church. What of the other situations? Each deserves lengthy consideration in its own right, and of course every church is unique and different; but we can attempt some generalisations which will need developing with local detail and colour.

A typical *city centre* church is often described as a stranded whale. Large congregations used to fill a capacious building, but development of the area has taken place and now a comparatively small number commute from the suburbs to maintain the witness. Once the domain of well-known preachers, few attend on Sundays, however good the standard of preaching may be. There is often a relevant mid-week ministry of caring, and in spite of the difficulties there is still a vital role for the preaching ministry. On the one hand, the city pulpit can still be a sounding board which speaks to city life, urging the biblical note of justice and offering a voice for those who have none of their own. On the other hand, there can be a personal proclamation. People *do* drop in, and when they do it is important that they should hear about a God whose love is for them. One city church was described as the 'box office' of its denomination. It was not a bad analogy in that it encouraged people to link up with their local church, once the initial contact had been made.

Part of the ministry of the city centre church ought to be that of prayer. When the Jews were exiled to Babylon, Jeremiah encouraged them to pray for the city to which they had gone, and commit themselves to it (chapter 29, especially verses 4-7, 11). The preacher can remind people and help them in this task.

The *inner city* church usually sees itself as the serving community, set in what is usually an area of immense deprivation. The visiting preacher will need to come as a learner, since it is hard to exercise empathy with the inner city unless one lives there. Fred Pratt Green has a marvellous phrase which pictures Christians as 'servants of the Servant'[3] and this well describes how many in the inner city feel about their ministry. A close study of the gospel story, with Jesus alongside people in their need and impatient with the aspirations of political (and religious!) leaders, sustains them in their work. That will be a sound basis for preaching, together with the wider themes of the Bible which speak of the richness of the life God offers and the growth in grace which he desires of his people.

The *suburban and town* churches are usually assumed to be the strength from which the denominations operate, probably because in general terms they are the best attended types of congregation, with corresponding financial stability. But those who belong to such churches make it clear that they too have their struggles, and a pulpit ministry of encouragement is needed as much here as elsewhere. So, given a fair-sized congregation, with all ages from nought to ninety-plus represented, it is possible to see that the scope for preaching ought to be extremely wide. For example, it can be easier and less demanding to belong to this kind of church: one may come in quietly and occupy an inconspicuous place. So there may well be need for challenge to deeper commitment. Similarly, it may be assumed that the larger church will be well-gifted. Just because people have a professional background does not mean that they will be more gifted as Christians; but there are probably many abilities and skills, as well as biblical gifts, that they possess and should be offering to church and neighbourhood. Growth in the Christian life is an important theme here, as elsewhere.

The *village* church is far from monochrome: it presents itself to us in a variety of forms. There are small wayside chapels, apparently in the middle of nowhere, which serve a group of scattered farms or even one or two large families; there are those set in genuinely rural communities, and there are those in villages which have been developed so that they are virtually dormitory areas or suburbs of a nearby town. In this third case, the congregation may be of fair size, and the preacher will have the feeling of being in a town church. Folk may not know each other very well, whereas in the truly rural situation people will know each other very well indeed. Their families will have lived near each other, depended on each other and done business with each other for generations.

Since many village churches are sadly able to look back on better days as far as numbers are concerned, the theme of encouragement will not be out of place. Where there has been an influx of new people, there may be some difficulty in the new and the old settling together, though this will not be the case everywhere, because many places have been delighted to receive the newcomers. But themes concerning relationships, such as acceptance, forgiveness and growing together, may be of relevance. Always we ought to remind people of the growth in faith and love to which they are called by Christ.

The variety of people and places to which the average preacher will go ought to be a stimulus to our work. It ought to be anything but monotonous, and if on occasion we do repeat a sermon, the experience will probably turn out quite differently as we seek to apply it in a different context.

One of our hymns invites us to see the Church in somewhat triumphalist terms:
> Like a mighty army
> Moves the Church of God.[4]

It may be difficult to think in this way if we are preaching to a dozen people in a building which could seat perhaps fifty times that number. But there are other pictures, one of them being Jesus' promise of being with the small group. There is also the rather more realistic theology of his encouragement to his first followers: 'Do not be afraid, little flock, for your Father has been pleased to give you the kingdom' (Luke 12:32). The emphasis on giving is important. We belong to a God who is gracious by nature: his essence is that of giving. That lights up and influences the way in which I set out to obey his call to preach.

6

MESSAGE AND WITNESS

Much of the variety of preaching will be pressed upon you: the churches you go to, the people you meet, perhaps the lectionary readings, will make their own demands. But it will lie in your own hands to work positively to find the best ways of using your opportunities.

Paul has an interesting phrase with which he tries to explain to the Christians in Corinth something of his motivation and tactics for his mission. He talks about having sought to be 'all things to all men' in his desire to share the grace of Christ (1 Corinthians 9:22).

We can release Paul from the possible charge that he had been a dissembler. His attitude was a long way from that of the shady politician who will tell you whatever he thinks you want to hear, in order to win your vote. Paul's aim had been always to act in complete openness and sincerity. What he was claiming was that he had attempted to understand all the groups and individuals to whom he had ministered. He could appreciate how Jewish people felt, having come from the same background, and he had taken pains to see things also from the Gentile point of view. Knowing the people, and their allegiances, he had then pointed to the sufficiency of Christ. There had been great variety in his ministry, but all to the same end.

We have been looking at ways in which variety of approach can enrich our preaching ministry. A final word needs to be said about how to keep the freshness in our work.

(1) We shall do well to keep up our reading, both in depth and breadth. There is a caution in 2 Timothy 3:7 about those who are always learning but never really discovering the truth. There are people who fall into that trap; but few of us are the kind of intellectuals who love nothing better than an argument, nor do we have time for unlimited study. What we may well do is seek to emulate some of the early Methodist preachers (many of them self-taught) who saw *any* reading as background preparation for their work in proclaiming the gospel. Read widely, and let the wonder of the world and its inhabitants enthuse your understanding of the Lord's creation; and read deeply, so that your appreciation of the Bible and theological matters may strengthen all that you say.

(2) Set yourself to be, like John Wesley, *homo unius libri* (a man – or woman – of one book). He read widely; he abridged others' works so that his followers could have good books readily available, and he brought it all to the light of the revelation of God to be found in the Bible. This book was a source of devotion, and the yardstick of all his thought.

We are often warned not simply to read the Bible as a source for sermons. It must be a book that speaks to us personally. The more we allow that to happen, the more we shall in fact have to share with others. A group of preachers was talking about themes for Harvest Festival services, and bemoaning the impression that they seemed limited in number. One person spoke up. He had found so many harvest themes that he did not think that he could ever use them all! He had soaked himself in the Old Testament, with positive results.

(3) Try to keep a sense of awe about what you are doing. Did you wonder, when you first began to preach, why the Lord had troubled to call someone like you? Never take your calling for granted. W. R. Maltby had a piece which he called 'A preacher's damnation': 'He spoke of great

things and made them small: of holy things and made them common: of God and made him of no account.' As you seek for variety in what you offer, it may in fact help you to keep the wonder and freshness there.

Part of that freshness will come from reflection on the facts of the faith. One of the best of modern hymns is 'We have a gospel to proclaim', by Edward J Burns.[1] It is a recital of the salvation offered in Christ, through the events of Bethlehem, Calvary, Easter, the Ascension and the coming of the Spirit. It is in the tradition of the catalogue that Paul set out in 1 Corinthians 15:3-5. Our faith, and our enthusiasm, are based on the story and present reality of God's activity.

(4) Be willing to accept criticism. It may be painful at times, but if it is constructive, it will be abundantly worthwhile. Most of us are used to being thanked at the church door. That thanks may be genuinely felt, or it may be merely an act of politeness. If it suggests that we have done well, it may be dangerous. Try to find two or three people, not all of the same viewpoint, who will meet with you occasionally to share their reactions to your preaching.

(5) It is also worth reading sermons, and of course listening to them. Preachers are supposed to be poor listeners, so it may be that we have to learn the art. We listen, not to steal others' ideas, but to get the feel of how they do things. We also listen as part of our worshipping! Some lay preachers said of one of their number that they valued his preaching and conduct of worship because it showed 'how it should be done'. They did not necessarily agree with everything, but they found in him a test for their own work.

(6) Part of the art of keeping your preaching fresh and varied is to remember, as we said when we began, that when we engage in Christian proclamation we are talking about a person rather than discussing ideas. Ideas matter, and must be expressed as clearly and attractively as possible, but we are in the event pointing to a person who is exercising his truth within his world. Phillips Brooks, much-loved hymn-

writer and preacher, made the point that as we prepare or actually preach, there should be two words constantly before us: message and witness.[2] We are to speak a message about the grace and love of God, seen in Jesus Christ. We are to witness that we know the message to be true, because it has become a force within our own lives. Such conviction ought to inspire immediacy and integrity in what we are saying.

(7) The final word, as it ought always to be for the preacher, should be about prayer. As we have considered how best to prepare sermons in a variety of ways, we have assumed throughout that the whole exercise will be conducted in a spirit of prayer. Yet prayer must never be taken for granted. It must be quite specific. I ought to be asking for the message to be given to me, for the hearers to be receptive, for God to be allowed to do whatever he wants in his service and sermon. What I say may be only mere words, unless the Lord breathes life into them through his Spirit.

NOTES

Chapter 1

1 James S Stewart, *A Faith to Proclaim*, Hodder & Stoughton, London 1946,

Chapter 2

1 See chapter 3.

2 Some scholars do not accept 2 Timothy as a genuine letter of Paul and would hesitate about this reference to Mark. But there is an argument for the position that even if Paul did not write this letter it contains genuine fragments of his words. Many will find no difficulty with this tribute to Mark.

3 See also chapter 5.

4 See also chapter 5.

Chapter 3

1 See the note in *The Methodist Worship Book*, Methodist Publishing House, Peterborough 1999, p.521.

2 See above, pp.26-27 regarding continuous and related readings.

3 Lion Publishing, Oxford.

4 F F Bruce, *This is That: The New Testament Development of Some Old Testament Themes*, Paternoster Press, London 1968, p.14.

5 James Black, *The Mystery of Preaching*, James Clarke, London 1934, pp.128-134.

6   Both published by Hodder & Stoughton, London.

7   Terry Waite, *Taken on Trust*, Hodder & Stoughton, London 1993.

Chapter 4

1   W E Sangster, *The Craft of Sermon Construction*, Epworth, London 1949, p.23.

2   J B Phillips, *The Book of Revelation*, Geoffrey Bles, London 1957.

3   Op. cit, p.33.

Chapter 5

1   *Hymns & Psalms*, Methodist Publishing House, 1983, no 540 v5.

2   *Hymns & Psalms*, no 572.

3   In the hymn, 'God is here!' *Hymns & Psalms*, no 653.

4   'Onward! Christian soldiers' by Sabine Baring-Gould. This verse is omitted in *Hymns & Psalms*, but may be found at no 822 in the 1933 *Methodist Hymn Book*.

Chapter 6

1   *Hymns & Psalms*, no 465.

2   Quoted in John W Doberstein, *The Minister's Prayer Book*, Collins, London 1964, pp.405-6.